Finding a Place

of

Peace

Finding a Place of Peace

DAWN VIRCKS

Dedication

To those whose lives were touched by Ryan

Acknowledgments

I thank Rachel for holding my other hand while God walked me through the process of writing my story. Your passion, Rachel, for serving others is beautiful and inspiring. I am grateful to have gained a daughter through this journey.

Words cannot portray how thankful I am for you, Helen! Thank you for using your gifts to serve our Lord who called us out of darkness into His glorious light. You saved me lots of unnecessary anguish.

I see the faithfulness and beauty of God in both of you women. Jesus with skin on.

Thank you, Lyn Cote, for your encouragement as I neared the end of the writing process.

I am grateful to Mark, Collette, and Robin for reading my story and offering your feedback.

Thank you, Thad, Austin, Brad, and my family who never ceased to love and support me.

Kitty, I am thankful for your willingness to share your pain with others. May your writings continue to inspire others as they have me.

There are so many others who walked with me to the place I am now! Thank you for your love and support.

Most of all, I thank you who prayed for our family during this season of life. We are at this place because of your prayers. You are the heroes in this story.

I love you all!

Chapter One

GOODBYE

IN LIFE EVERYTHING HAS ITS GOODBYES
EVERYTHING MUST LEAVE AT SOMETIME,
FOR WHEN SOMEONE SAYS A GOODBYE
TO SOMEONE OR SOME THING,
THEY ARE FOCUSING ON THE GOODBYE, THE PRESENT,
LOOK AT THE PAST NOT THE PRESENT,
LOOK AT EVERYTHING THAT THAT PERSON/THING WAS,
WHAT THEY OR IT MEANT TO YOU,
WHEN YOU SAY GOODBYE YOU TURN YOUR HEAD AND
WALK AWAY,
WELL DON'T TURN YOUR HEAD BUT KEEP ON LOOKING ON,
GOODBYES ARE NOTHING BUT EXISTENCE IS EVERYTHING.
GOODBYE.

-Ryan
4-23-97

No one has seen our oldest son Ryan since he left his high school yesterday afternoon. He is a junior there, well-liked by other kids, funny and introspective.

My husband Noel, my sister Jan, and I are in the kitchen. I'm cleaning up after lunch. Noel and Jan are chatting casually. One of them mentions the fact that there was a bank robbery yesterday in our town of Cedar Rapids, Iowa—a mid-sized city.

"It can't be him," I chime in, "because Ryan doesn't have white tennis shoes."

I blurted this out because that was the first thing that went through my mind the day before when I saw the image of the bank robber on the news. The only part of him showing was his feet clad in white tennis shoes.

YESTERDAY
April 30, 1997

Ryan came home around noon. He stood behind me and said, "Let's go out for lunch!"

He was in a very happy mood. I couldn't go with him because I had an appointment to get my hair cut.

So he went by himself and had lunch at Long John Silver's. When he came back he went up to his room in the loft. As I prepared to leave I hollered up, "Do you need anything from the grocery store? I'm going there after I get my hair cut."

He replied that he didn't need anything. I wondered why because he loved to eat, as any teenage boy does, and usually asked for the food he liked. But off I went.

Groceries and haircuts. Normal, mundane conversations between a mother and teenaged son. These interactions happen every day all over the world, a million times over. Totally normal. When I came back from the grocery store I had food to put away. And I had to pick Austin, Ryan's seven-year-old brother, up from school. As I shelved the groceries I saw a note on the table.

"Mom, went to Kyle. I will probably eat over with him 2" There was a picture on the side that looked like a cartoon clown with a hole in his forehead. Fear gripped my heart for a sliver of a second. He hadn't signed "Ryan" as he usually did but instead his full name.

Should I call Kyle? I felt uncertain about the voice niggling my subconscious. I didn't want to be a helicopter mother who can't stand a second away from her kids. I was torn. I didn't know if I should finish putting the groceries away and get to Austin's school on time to pick him up. Or call Kyle? If we had cell phones back then I would have texted Ryan.

It was only a couple minutes before 3:00 p.m. so I thought, I'll call later if I can't get rid of this feeling.

During all this "thinking" I drove to get Austin. He sometimes had trouble during transitions—going to school, coming home, getting ready for dinner, bedtime. Each of these things caused him a certain amount of angst. This day though, when I picked him up he fell apart, like I'd never seen him do. He screamed, yelled, and cried. I couldn't get him to stop. It was like this little boy knew something was up.

I don't know if Austin felt it, but as we drove away from his school in the heavy rain the "something's up" went from being a phrase in my head to becoming a bottomless pit in my heart. By the time we got home, one storm was over—the physical storm of wind and rain. But the other—the proverbial emotional storm of my life—continued.

Noel unexpectedly dropped by in the middle of his UPS delivery route, bringing a black plastic bag with two baby rabbits inside. He acted all tenderhearted, loving and emotional. Very unusual behavior for the middle of his workday. One bunny died within a few hours; the other hung on to life. The kids and I tried to find a way to feed the tiny bunny in order to keep it alive. By caring for the animals briefly, my mind was distracted from the storm raging in my soul.

Ryan's friend Kyle called. "Is Ryan home?" he asked. His voice was very different from his usual voice. It seemed like another validation that something was dreadfully wrong.

We figured that any minute Ryan would come bounding in the door as he usually did, his brain bursting with ideas for his next homemade movie or story. Ryan had a boundless imagination, and he was well-liked by everyone.

As afternoon turned into evening we still had no idea where Ryan was. I took the initiative to call the police. The police said we could not file a missing persons report until Ryan had been gone for 24 hours.

During this time, Noel told me he was going to go to work the next morning. "You are NOT going to work!" I responded, surprised by the passion in my voice. I knew I needed him to be home. I just didn't know why.

We gave Ryan a little bit more time to come home. We didn't want to go through his room, poking around and rifling through his things. But a point came when we no longer cared about upsetting him.

When we entered his room it was clear he had cleaned it up like someone who was ready to move. Ryan had taken his bed down a few weeks earlier (one loaned to him by his friend Cody) and stored it at his grandparents' home. Without a bed in his room he had placed a large piece of linoleum over part of the carpet. He said that was so that he could have a dance floor to practice break dancing, and he slept on the carpeting.

There in the middle of the floor were his school books in a perfect stack. It was so odd. He had never done anything like that before. On the top was a poem he had written for us—the Goodbye poem that opened this chapter.

He said goodbye. My heart sank to a depth I had never felt before. However, as night fell I had a strange sense of calm and a knowing that I would need the sleep the night afforded me. The 24 hours for filing the missing person report would be up tomorrow. Some parents may have gone out looking for their child. Something told me this was not going to work. All I could do was go to bed. My body would need the rest for the following days.

THE NEXT DAY
May 1, 1997

When I awoke around 5:00 a.m. I laid there praying, talking to God. "What am I going to do, God?"

Call your sister.

"But it's too early to call her," I argued. Still I asked again, "What am I going to do?"

Call your sister Jan was His patient answer.

When I called Jan I told her that Ryan was missing.

"I have a meeting to go to this morning," she replied. I gulped. I had done what God told me to do. I hung up the phone.

Seconds later Jan called back. "I'm not going to that meeting! I'll be there in a couple of hours." Jan was my anchor. She knew exactly what to do next. In big ways and small all through the crazy hours that followed, Jan loved me in a way only she could. She seemed to know what I needed before I needed it.

Meanwhile, Kyle called to tell us he had found Ryan's car. I stopped by there on my way to take Austin to school. The car was parked on the street behind a local church in a residential area. My heart went to my shoes again when I saw it.

I just want to die, I thought. I knew something was terribly wrong. Austin, sitting next to me in the passenger seat, spoke bringing me back to reality.

I can't die, I thought, looking at Austin. I had to make a conscious decision right then and there to stay alive so I could help Austin and Thad survive. My younger sons needed me.

In that moment I decided that Austin would be my reason for living. One son was off somewhere. I would pour all my energies into the two who remained, especially this youngest boy—only seven years old. I had the gut feeling Thad would survive. He was almost fourteen at the time, had a good head on his shoulders, and a well-rounded heart. This new world made no sense, but surely I could keep Austin safe.

Intuitively I knew that life was going to be different.

MY SISTER ARRIVES

Jan arrived at our house around 8:30 a.m. Jan had been a private investigator for twenty-some years, specializing in criminal cases. She had never done any domestic cases.

She sat down and started going through all the facts with me—already investigating. "Let's go interview people," she finally said. Jan has a gift. She knows what people need and she gives it to them. She intercedes for others. She's a go-getter.

We started with a list of Ryan's friends. She and I went to the friend's house near where I found Ryan's car parked. We were slightly worried that because no one answered the door they might be asleep or passed out. We peeked in to see. There was no sign of life anywhere. In fact, we didn't find a single person home on the friends list.

"We're going to the school," Jan said. She went in to the administrative office at the high school. All business. It didn't take much convincing for the principal to allow us to talk to those who knew Ryan best. We talked to three friends including his girlfriend, Leah. None gave any indication that they sensed anything amiss.

Toward lunchtime we arrived back home. Feeling frustrated but still functioning pretty normally, I fixed lunch. Noel came home. He had been out searching too. Jan had her suspicions. We were all just trying to get information.

Jan called her husband. "Listen, we've looked everywhere and there is no sign of Ryan," she said. The authorities still did not know the identity of the ski-mask-wearing bank robber. I couldn't hear the other side of Jan's phone conversation but assumed her husband had said she should investigate further.

"But Dawn is adamant it's not him," she said. "The shoes aren't Ryan's." She got off the phone and spoke to me. "Dawn, I have to call the police."

She looked square into my eyes and said, "Are you ready?"

We had the same "knowing" pass between us that we had as sisters from early on. But I still didn't let the "knowing-in-my-gut" part move to my head. It was the emotional equivalent of taking a big breath before doing something you dread. We never actually expressed words that indicated either of us thought Ryan was the bank robber.

Jan's phone call was the catalyst for the police department to connect the dots—they had a young man in their morgue, and this family had a missing child.

Five minutes later the phone rang. It was the police department calling back for Jan.

"I'm at the parents' house right now," she said.

FINDING OUT

Seconds later, it seemed, two officers knocked at the door. I thought they had come to file a police report on Ryan being missing for over 24 hours.

We sat down at the dining room table.

"I'd like to talk to Noel first," one officer said. The two of them and Noel went into the living room. Jan and I stayed in the dining room.

Jan remembers and will never forget the wail from deep down in his soul that Noel let out. She watched my eyes flash for a second and then I was mentally gone. In shock. She grabbed hold of me, but I just sat and stared. Shortly, I became aware of my surroundings again. We were still sitting at the table.

"What are they doing?" I asked her. She didn't answer. Deep in my heart I knew I really didn't want to know that Ryan was dead.

Noel came back into the room with the police officers. They let him be the one to tell me. "Ryan robbed the bank," he said. He didn't show me the picture in his hand that identified Ryan's body.

I needed proof. I needed something to make this all real. I turned to my sister. "Is it true that Ryan is the one who robbed the bank?"

"Yes," she said. "Ryan is the one who robbed the bank."

I simply needed someone to tell me it was true. The powerful force of denial was at work while shock was protecting me.

If this is true, why am I not crying? I thought. What is wrong with me? I didn't feel anything. I remember wandering around and settling on the front steps of the house. Nothing was clear. It was like being in a deep space—a black hole. Right when I needed someone who was like an anchor in my life, Jan was there. I had a sudden feeling though that I needed to tell my next door neighbor Becky about what was going on. I felt like I couldn't move off the steps until I talked to her.

"We need to be going soon to identify his body," one of the police officers said. "The press will be coming. They will want to cover the story."

I felt like I was swimming through glue. I asked the officer to knock on Becky's front door and ask her to come over. She ran in our direction. As I watched her, my emotions began to connect to this strange new reality. The way she ran, her posture, the look on her face—nothing was right. What I had known in my heart began to connect with my brain.

Becky sat next to me on the front steps. She said nothing but was a calming presence. Ironically, some children celebrating the happy first day of May came by with May baskets. Perhaps they expected to knock on our door and run. But there we sat in a shattered world—me in shock and Becky trying to figure out what to do to help.

THE HOSPITAL

One of the officers takes us to the hospital so we can make an in-person, positive identification of our son's body. Arriving, we enter a small room. A priest or clergyman is there. His words give me something to hang on to. They are an anchor, a calming noise in a screaming void. I don't want him to stop talking. The resonance of his vocal chords off the walls of this small room keep me from flying into space. I know he is God's human manifestation of love to me. This man is God's grace to me. My daily bread. Oh, how I need it!

The police officers come back and tell us Ryan's body has been lying in the morgue for 22-24 hours. They have been waiting for someone to identify him.

Ryan was my sweet, firstborn son with bright red hair. In this same hospital his blue eyes had opened wide almost seventeen years earlier—wide in indignation and anger as he wailed his insolence at being born. Then as the doctor held him up for me to see, Ryan peed on me. Like a ritual of baptism.

Now in the same building I see my precious son at the end of his life.

My boy, my boy, my boy.

I know I am facing the hardest thing I have ever, or will ever, have to face. Yet my feet keep walking to where my son is waiting.

"Yes," I said when asked if I wanted to see his body. "Yes, I need to see him or I won't believe this is real."

A door creaks in protestation.

Oxygen leaves the room.

Noel and I walk into this sacred space to look at the body in which our first son's soul once resided. Lying there, it is apparent that a bullet has torn through one of his eyes. It is gone. The other eye is open, staring. Here is one beautiful blue eye and that red hair. My boy.

I am overwhelmed by the immensity, a swallowing-me-whole feeling and a palpable, gnawing loss. I can't breathe. All the hopes and dreams I had for this boy! Each and every day I had prayed to God for his safety and God's protection on his life.

I do not comprehend. I crouch down near his head. I whisper to him, simultaneously breathing in his smell. Memories flood my mind. Trips to Colorado, silly videos made and edited with friends, Ryan always leading the charge. Memories of him scooching out of his stroller and flipping onto the ground at two weeks of age. The gentle way he had with his younger brothers.

Memories fight with the present. My heart is shattered.

"Do you have any idea how much I love you?" I croak. I am close to his head and crying into his hair. Crying so hard. I look at his body in the hospital gown. Here lies my hopes and dreams. Alone. Exposed. Gone.

Ryan had cut his knee open a few years before, and during the autopsy they opened up that scar. That makes me angry. He is already so full of bullets. They said he was shot 13 times. Why did they have to cut that open too? Why can't you just leave him alone? my heart cries to everyone and to no one and to the shiny steel instruments sitting at attention on the counter.

"Why did you have to do it?" Noel says from the other side of the gurney.

The wall clock answers us. Its incessant ticking reminds us that time is still marching on and we will be forced to return to a world in which Ryan does not exist. I think, *I could spend the rest of my life in this room and it wouldn't be long enough.* But I must go and leave him in this place with the clock and the instruments.

Beauty from ashes. I kiss him. And I close the stubborn blue eye of that stubborn boy. *You know what son? I'm your mother. When you were born you were crying and you peed on me. Now you're silent in death and I get to close your eye.*

That is my final act of service to my son. A son who had been prayed for, loved, and raised in a Christian home. A last act of love for his physical body.

We have about ten minutes in that room. Who can know that my heart wants to stop?

The police tell us that we need to get back to our house. The media will soon be arriving. Our devastation is about to become dinner-table discussion for others.

At home the media is swarming.

But another difficult job awaits us—telling Ryan's brothers what happened. Thad and Austin are waiting. Noel explains to the boys that Ryan had been killed while robbing a bank. He is able to show the kids his emotional pain while hugging them.

My heart is a wall of ice. I feel numb—if numbness can be felt. I sit racking my brain, trying to connect my emotions to the truth. I feel like I am in front of an emotional vending machine. The lever I would have pulled was *You will die now.* Foreign emotions. Which was appropriate? I have never been in this impossible situation before. I have never hoped or expected to be.

From this day forward we would raise two children. The joy of parenting Ryan was over. No longer would Thad and Austin have a big brother to mentor them. I struggle to wrap my head around the truth that my reluctant heart is already feeling and beginning to understand.

All of this and it's still May 1st.

Chapter Two

LAYING RYAN TO REST

As I wake up to see the light is gone
just as I bow my head
It's too late for I know my time is gone.
What does it matter when we're gone?
What kind of difference/impact did we make?
What is our role in this story of life?
Is all I'm worth a few tears and a little sorrow?

-Ryan

Noel and I attended to the details of picking out a casket and a headstone. We decided where the service would be held and what time. It's strange when the freshness of grief falls over you. You want to do everything within your power to control what you can. You don't want to seem cheap when you're burying your child.

It was tempting to buy more for him. But we chose a simple wooden casket with a cream inlay. I really wanted blue next to him, so my friend Laura bought a powder-blue sheet, and the funeral director laid it under his body.

My dad had bought a couple extra cemetery lots. His dad and mom (my grandparents) had worked at Cedar Memorial Cemetery—my grandmother in the flower shop and my grandfather mowing for them on a part-time basis. One day my grandfather was mowing under a tree and his hat was knocked off by a low limb.

"This is where I want to be buried," he said. So he bought those lots. His daughter and her husband bought lots next to them, and my parents bought lots near those. My dad bought three extra lots in case someone died prematurely or had a baby who was stillborn. Ryan would be here at seventeen instead of seventy-one, part of that family plot formed beneath the tree.

I always believed that when a child dies you're supposed to let someone else speak. But Noel wanted to talk to Ryan's friends and to the media. I, on the other hand, wanted to be more quiet, to be allowed to grieve in my own way and on my own timeline.

Once we got to the church I took Austin to be with some kids he knew. That was something normal for me to do. One little boy from our church was there for Austin to talk to.

When he and Austin were two and three years old, they had been dressed as angels in the church's Christmas pageant. They looked almost exactly alike. Noel had brought our video camera, and he started filming who he thought was Austin. It turned out it was the other little boy. We always called him "pretend Austin" after that.

So thinking of that event on this horrific day lent a moment of levity. Normality in a sea of sorrow. Death all around, and these two little guys chatting as though everything was the same as yesterday. It was a reminder to all of us that life was going to go on. And it might just be okay.

THE FUNERAL SERVICE

We chose Ryan's guitar teacher Billy Heller to sing at the service. Ryan looked up to him so much. He chose to play Eric Clapton's "Tears in Heaven" on Ryan's guitar as a special memorial. He even left Ryan's rusty strings on the guitar so it sounded the same as it had the last time Ryan played.

Billy shared with us that one night when he and Ryan were working on that very song Ryan asked him if one of the chords he played was correct. Billy said he realized that it wasn't the right chord. He was astonished at Ryan's quick ear and adept hand with music.

I could see the people at the funeral service were hurting and needing answers. Sixteen- and seventeen-year-old kids staring death in the face. I desperately wanted them to feel hope. Noel saw this as an opportunity to share our faith with all who attended. He wanted something positive to come out of Ryan's death.

Two pastors spoke at the service: our friend and church worship pastor who lived next door and Ryan's youth pastor. They both did a wonderful job of showing God's love to the people in attendance. We wanted the gospel message to come through loud and clear so that God could redeem this mess and be glorified in the midst of it. And then Ryan's friend Scott hit the ball out of the park!

SCOTT CARSON SPEAKS AT THE SERVICE

"First I'd like to thank all of the people who have been praying for me to be able to speak today.

"One of my favorite memories of Ryan was when we went to a creek down at the end of my road. We took a sling-shot to hunt small animals. Ryan had my sling-shot, and when he fell in the creek he dropped it. The current swept it away. I should have been mad at him, but I couldn't be. He sat there in the water laughing his head off. That was one of my favorite things about him. You couldn't get mad because he was so funny.

"My name is Scott Carson. I have been a friend of Ryan's ever since we were little kids. I go to Solon High School, but I belong to the same youth group as Ryan did at New Covenant Bible Church.

"Growing up with Ryan I always looked up to him. He was a year older than me and I wanted to be like him. Ryan always had the best sense of humor and ability to make people laugh any time he was around. Ryan was the most selfless person I knew. He always thought of other people first. Having known Ryan for so long, the news of his death was devastating to me. It has been very difficult dealing with his death, but I have held on to one truth to help me through this time. I know Ryan is in Heaven with Jesus right now—no pain, no suffering, and no more troubles. I know this because Ryan is a born-again Christian. He asked Jesus into his heart, and by the blood of Jesus all of his sins have been washed clean and forgotten. The biggest reason I looked up to Ryan was because of his relationship with God. Ryan loved to praise God and play his guitar for Him. He often talked to me about being in God's presence during worship events, Bible studies, and Christian concerts. Ryan had a good relationship with God and his future was extremely bright—until he started to drift away. When you drift from God only bad things will happen. Ryan's life ended tragically because he had drifted far from God. Ryan chose to follow the things of the world which are contrary to God's will. God doesn't love Ryan any less because of the path he chose, but his choices cost him many of the good things God had planned for him on this earth.

"Ryan loved the Lord Jesus Christ and is in Paradise with him now. Not because Ryan attended church. Not because he gave his time and talent to serve on mission trips. Not because his mom and dad are Christians. But because he personally invited Jesus Christ into his life to be his Savior and Lord. The Bible tells us in Ephesians 2:8-9: 'For by grace you have been saved through faith, and that not of yourself, it is the gift of God; not as a result of works that no one should boast.'

"My memories of Ryan aren't going to be of a person who was straying from God. They will be of the real Ryan. The one who was on fire for God. The Ryan who loved to be in His presence praising Him. The Ryan who just like his mom and dad loved telling other people about Christ. That is the real Ryan. The Ryan who right now wants each of you who don't know the peace, love, and joy of Christ to invite Him into your life. That is the Ryan I will meet in Heaven some day."

THE INTERMENT

We rode as a family to the cemetery for the interment ceremony. I remember thinking, This is so surreal. So surreal.

It was a beautiful spring day. As the pastor talked my mind wandered. I wondered, Is this where Grandma and Grandpa are buried? Are we standing on them? Such a strange thought this day. My shocked brain was still trying to function on a very basic level. I thank God for that protective mechanism He gave us to undergo really horrible situations.

Again I thought, It is so cool that so many people are here. The people I could see next to us and all around us were grieving with us, showing us they cared.

After the pastor concluded his words he said, "The family would like each of you to take a rose from the casket spray."

What?

I got the wind knocked out of me. Like getting the news of losing Ryan all over again. The pastor had not talked to us about this. I was choking as people began to come forward to get a rose, feeling like they were taking a part of my son. I wanted every piece of him I could possibly keep. How could the pastor offer to give away those flowers?

I gotta think about this. Look at all these people. All of them taking a flower. No!

But in *that* moment I made a decision. I said to myself, "I want to give them a piece of Ryan."

I picked up the flowers and began to hand them to the

people who were more timid. I am glad I was able to do that and that everyone could have a reminder of him. I started to enjoy passing them out. It was as if I said, "If I can't do anything to make this better for you who are hurting so much, I can at least give you a rose."

There is nothing I love more than flowers. It ended up being a blessing to me and to others.

I forgave the pastor then and there.

Chapter Three

LOSSES & BLESSINGS

Sometimes it's sad that we can lose so much,
lose a feeling, lose a friend,
lose because of our laziness.
It's sad to see laziness wastes time because
that time will never return. It is gone.
Laziness is a disease that is curable
but the longer someone has it the more
hopeless it is to cure.
Pick yourself up now before it's too late.

Ryan's journal entry — 07/15/96

*S*hortly after Ryan's death, our neighbors the Klingbeils moved to Arizona. My best friend Laura moved to Oklahoma a week after Ryan's funeral. I had walked with another neighbor, Marlene, at least five times a week. She was a wonderful friend and support for me as we talked over our motherhood experiences. She moved that summer as well. I was very close to all three of these women. Now they were gone—all within a few weeks' time.

Having these neighbors gone was another loss. These people I had depended on to help me through the days with their accepting presence and their little kindnesses were no longer there. I felt lonelier than ever before.

I spent the month after Ryan's death going through the

motions and reading the nice cards and letters people had sent us. The huge hole in my heart was painful. It was with me, unwanted, wherever I went. When would the pain subside? How would it happen? Sometimes I suffered with the fear that it would never go away.

I decided I had to trust God to make something good happen at this point in my life. I prayed for Him to send me a friend. God does send people when we need them, whether we recognize it at the time or not. Sometimes they are neighbors or acquaintances, sometimes people who see a need and fill it.

People sometimes think they have to do a really grand gesture in the life of a grieving person when often all that is needed to make a difference is to just show up or offer your help with something you're good at.

Carol Akey was the direct answer to that prayer for a friend. She was the woman God sent me to help ease the burden of an aching heart. Carol was a busy lady, homeschooling her children while running a home business. It was gracious of her to take the time to be my friend. She called me out of the blue one day. "Would you like to start walking with me?" she asked. And that was that. We started praying together every morning as we walked. She was there for me in the midst of my deepest hurt. She listened.

HURTS BECOME LOSSES

SHAME: "Do you feel ashamed of Ryan for what he did?" I was actually asked this question. I remember thinking, I'm not going to be ashamed of my son. I'm going to hold my head high. I'm going to grieve like I need to grieve. I had no illusions about what I would be up against. I needed to be true to myself and not let other peoples' opinions of Ryan affect my memories of him and our life together.

CRYING: Another "take" by people on the outside

looking in when they see you crying is "Oh, I don't think she's doing very well." I believe crying showed others how much Ryan meant to me. At a celebration of life service at the end of an elderly person's long life you're happy because they've lived a long, full life. For Ryan, we felt that his life was cut short. So his funeral wasn't really a celebration. Of course we cried.

CHILD SELECTION: "You still have two other children." So we shouldn't grieve the loss of our son because we have two others? Losing one is no big deal? I wanted to ask this person, "If you had to pick which child you could live without, which one would you pick?"

ISOLATION: The kids at Ryan's school wanted to plant a tree in his memory. One of the parents thought that would be a bad thing—planting a tree for someone who had died committing a crime. I think they wondered what kind of message it would send to other kids.

That hurt! It made me feel even more ostracized and isolated from the parents at school.

BAD PARENTING: My neighbor Becky said if a kid does a bad thing, do not judge by coming to the conclusion that his parents obviously did something wrong. Kids don't come with guarantees.

PROJECTING: Well-meaning friends and relatives will say, "When you get to Heaven you'll know all the answers." At that point, I think, I won't care. It will be a moot point because I will hold my son in my arms after long years without him. I don't think I will care why he robbed the bank and caused his own death. I believe God created a perfect place for those who love Him. When we arrive, there will be no more sorrow. God will wipe away all our tears. I don't believe I will even have a memory of the pain we suffered.

INFECTIOUS: Who would think that because a little boy's brother had died under unusual circumstances it would be catching?

When Noel and I separated and I moved with the boys to a different home, a little boy who lived across the street played with Austin. His sister who was Thad's age told her mom what had happened to Ryan. After that Austin wasn't allowed to play with her son.

When I spoke to her I said, "I can understand why you might be fearful, but could Austin come over to play when you're home?"

Her feelings didn't have anything to do with Austin. Still she wouldn't allow him to play there. "You're a much stronger person than I am," she said. I think she meant because I wasn't angry with her. I was respectful. Ryan's passing away presented treacherous territory that she wasn't ready to deal with. She simply wanted to keep her kids safe and couldn't seem to do it any other way.

This was another kind of loss—not only for me, but for Austin. Suffering that consequence was one of the most painful things I went through.

BEAUTY FOR ASHES

Not everything is negative when you lose someone you love. There are wonderful, thoughtful people who touch your life for a moment and cause you to be thankful in the midst of the sorrow. A simple act of service performed at just the right time has the power to transform the raw loss of suffering into a kind of hope—hope that family and friends would help carry us through.

The memories which follow are in no particular order—simply blessings that I remember and how they helped me to cope.

On that fateful day when we learned about Ryan's crime and his death, my neighbor Becky was the person who urged our Christian brothers and sisters throughout the city to pray for us. This was only the beginning of a beautiful tapestry. The threads used to weave it were the prayers by the faithful on our behalf. There is no way to repay that kind of giving.

She told me later that a woman from our church had been cooking dinner for her family that night. When she heard about Ryan on the radio she brought that full meal over for us. And Becky herself realized as our house filled up with people that we would need more ice. She went to the store for it so the people who had come to support us would have ice for their drinks.

Other friends appeared. One young girl washed my dishes.

Ryan's commission of this crime was an enormous shock. No one had any idea Ryan was capable of doing something like this. Or that he was desperate enough to do it. They just found it so hard to imagine that this act was within his capacity.

Memories from the day of Ryan's funeral came to me later. I remember a friend from high school whom I hadn't seen for many years stood in the back and gave me a big hug.

Another friend, Maureen, took Austin to deliver the May baskets we had assembled the night before.

Bill Heller, who played Ryan's guitar at the funeral service, poured out his love in that act of service. It meant so much.

I remember that the pastor's wife Sharon stood near the door as the pallbearers carried the casket out. I looked at her and said, "He's not there." She nodded in affirmation as if she knew I needed to say that to someone, maybe even to hear myself say it aloud. It was an important step, bringing me closer to reality. I felt peace for that moment, knowing we both understood that this world isn't our final resting place.

Friends who let me talk about anything one day—and who allowed me to be silent the next—were renewing for me.

People in our church went out of their way to do kind things. The mother of Austin's friend brought a big, delicious salad.

Another friend asked me what I needed help with. I remember she scrubbed my kitchen floor.

"What helps?" another woman who had several boys at Austin's school asked. What an amazing thing to ask someone who is hurting. It was one of the sweetest things anyone said to me, and I have never forgotten it. I answered, "What you just said helps."

ONE YEAR LATER

One island of emotional respite on the one-year anniversary of Ryan's death was the kind gesture of friends who loaned us the use of their home in Galena, IL for the weekend. It was lovely and gave us a time away from many things we didn't have the words for or were afraid to face. There were emotional land-mines everywhere. Ryan's favorite food at the grocery store. A piece of his clothing. Something funny that happened that I wanted to tell him about. That split-second of starting to call up to his loft bedroom before I remembered and the black curtain of loss dropped over my heart again.

When we came home from Galena we found a little garden in front of our house that a group of our friends had participated in. In it was a bird bath, nice plants, and a statue of a little boy by a fire hydrant. We had a tiny yard, so the friend who put it together had to be creative. Seeing that garden when we got home was a gift. She sent a beautiful message of love in my love language. This garden meant hope to me. We have pictures of Thad and Austin and our new puppy in front of it.

Following is a letter we received shortly after Ryan's death which touched our hearts deeply. We did not know this young man.

To your family:

I'm nineteen years old and presently incarcerated at the Linn County Correctional Center. My ignorance and drinking almost caused the death of another young man. It's very hard knowing my actions almost caused this. I continue breaking my heart by thinking of the pain I caused this family. I was not trying to seriously hurt this young man but that's what happened.

My point is that this trying time I'm going through has given me a greater love and compassion for all living things. My two younger brothers attend Washington High School. I also attended Washington. My brothers knew your son better than I. I had just seen him. He was always quiet, cheery, and amongst decent people. I usually don't write people I don't know but I believe God gave me the idea for this poem and then He wanted me to send it to you.

It's unexplainable why God took your son from you. I'm sure He has something up his sleeve. You probably feel like the pain will never go away but all it takes is time. All difficulties and evil in the world are conquered as soon as one conquers time. Please find good out of this tragic incident, maybe it will show kids that the glory of crime is only in the movies. I understand people must follow their own path to learn experience, but this will open some eyes.

Don't let anyone think your son was a criminal, he just got caught up in society's backwards hero-making. I don't see how you can tell kids not to steal when they're given role-models like John Dillinger and Jesse James. Their lives shouldn't be portrayed as glamorous, they should be shown for what they were, crooks. I think God may be using your son to help get this point across.

I want your family to know that I feel for you. The last two days I couldn't keep tears out of my eyes. This is a horrible tragedy that happened to such a beautiful kid. For some reason I feel you're a beautiful family and I can't help but to tell you I love you, and if there's anything I can do for you please know I'm here. I'm so sorry this had to happen to you.

Love Jerime

Jerime had only *seen* Ryan in the hall at their school, yet he felt this love for Ryan and shared it with us by sending this heartfelt letter and his poem. Jerime's words came from a place of suffering and sorrow from his own similar circumstances brought on by drinking.

Beautiful child set ablaze
sun shining on your soul,
with your vision in a haze
stumbled into the worlds darkest hole
Society open your eyes to a horrid surprise
you are the prince of thieves
sixteen years of age, caught in your web of deceit
you stole his reality
so accept your defeat-
Look and you shall see
you make their tale one of glory's
scandalous "saints" in romantic stories
we are all to blame
let's palm our shame-
Struggle'n to understand why your days came to cease
wanting you to still be here
here to stay-
with all my love
I'm wishin' I'd been the one gone away.
Dear delicate child rest in peace.

-Jerime '97

Jerime alludes to the fact that crime is tempting because it is glorified by society. Others may feel this way too, but I don't. I didn't teach my kids that kind of thinking. But Jerime makes a good point. Though this book is my version, every person who knew Ryan could come up with their own understanding of Ryan's life and why he did what he did.

You never know what kind of an impact you will have just by sending a note. Showing up. Being there. Bringing a meal. Some people don't know what to say. It is awkward for them, just as it was for me. They felt like they couldn't help. But because of what my friends and neighbors had done for me, I knew they were wrong.

It has always been difficult for me to accept help from people. I had to humble myself and learn that I didn't always need to be in control.

I've filed my own experiences as "the griever" away in my brain for the days when I see someone else grieving. Now that I've been there, I know how it feels and I know what helped me—what might possibly help someone else.

And you keep on living. Celebrating holidays. Watering flowers. Moving limbs that groan in protest. Trying to breathe. That's what you do when one of your children is gone.

Chapter Four

LOOKING BACK

Every moment in your life
is a <u>chance</u> to change.
To the better or the worse
or to stay the same.
It is for you to decide.
Realize your choices.

-Ryan's journal entry

I'm writing this chapter to show that we were a normal family with normal growing pains and normal struggles.

I met Noel at Bugsy's, an Al Capone-themed bar. You actually entered the bar down a slide, and the wait staff sported fake guns and rounds of ammo zipping across their chest. I was nineteen years old, fresh to the world, and a bit naïve.

I danced, the music mesmerizing and the moving tiles of light taking me to another place. We noticed each other as we danced, but we hadn't spoken to each other. Later as I walked out of the bathroom, this handsome man with wild seventies hair and a wonderful smile pulled me onto his lap and kissed me.

I had known who Noel was in high school, but I always thought he was a wild guy. He was confident, funny, and vivacious. I felt really noticed, like all the lights in the room had gone off except the spotlight shining on me. I felt like *somebody* when I was with him.

Our relationship was rocky. But the twin sister of tumult is passion. We were young and in love. We figured getting married would solve all of our relational problems.

OUR FIRST CHILD IS BORN

Two years later, and a few days after my due date passed, I finally went into labor. After several hours my contractions got stronger.

"I know your contractions hurt," said the nurse, "but they aren't progressing enough for you to have this baby."

During a few of my contractions the baby literally pushed back and up against the contraction. I could see the ripples on my abdomen. How odd was that? The first two times it happened the nurse wasn't in the room. At twenty-three, I didn't have any prior experience so I just thought it was odd.

The third time it happened the nurse saw it and a surprised look registered on her face. I can only describe it as my soon-to-be firstborn was reluctant to come into this world.

During his birth, before he was fully born the doctor said, "It has red hair!"

I didn't believe him, thinking, Why wouldn't the doctor know that was blood?

But when he held the wailing baby up, he was right. He did indeed have bright red hair! And at that moment, the little guy peed on me. We named him Ryan Noel.

Two weeks after Ryan was born he exhibited a strong will. Stubbornness. As I prepared to join my family for a game of tennis, I laid him in the stroller. He began an angry cry and got so mad that scooting his way to the end of the stroller (not a child-safe stroller like today's models) he flipped himself out. Two weeks old!

At the age of two and still strong-willed, he loved to

challenge and defy me, trying out the boundaries. One evening while I fixed supper Ryan touched and kept touching a large antique tree saw that hung on the wall as décor. I scolded him whenever he came near it and said, "No, no. Don't touch."

When I turned my back he snuck up to the saw and touched it again, giggling as he ran away. After several minutes of playing this game and seeing my stern reaction, I thought he understood the seriousness of touching the hanging saw.

I went back to the kitchen to finish cooking. When I checked on Ryan a few moments later, once again he was touching the saw. I stood frozen in place, horrified, as I watched this tree saw fall toward Ryan's little red head.

In what seemed like slow motion, the giant tool came toward his face. Then a sudden blur or mist, the color of distant clouds, came between Ryan and the saw. It came near his face and touched his cheek. Then it moved back slightly toward the wall and hung there for a moment.

Ryan reached out as if to hold the saw. It actually looked like he was being shown where to hold it until his mom got there to take it from him. He held it for a moment. I realized then it *could not* have been Ryan's strength holding it up. Something or someone was supernaturally holding the weight of the saw.

I hurried toward him and calmly took the saw from his little hand. His precious face registered surprise, and I felt an unexplained peace come over me during this time.

Ryan was too young to tell what he saw. But I knew without a doubt that my two-year-old son had been divinely protected. The tiniest mark made by the saw's tooth appeared on his right cheek—not even enough to cause bleeding. A tiny scar remained there for several years.

I thought of that miracle often throughout Ryan's life. It

was such a visual reminder of the protection over him of which I had no control.

SECOND SON BORN

Our second son Thad was a happy-go-lucky boy from day one. "Love me. Let's go play," seemed to be his constant mantra. He brimmed with carefree joy.

I don't remember Ryan and Thad ever fighting, though they probably poked and teased each other. I do remember that as a toddler Thad loved to have Ryan wrestle with him. Since Ryan didn't want to hurt him, he'd lay down pillows for protection.

When I was pregnant with Austin Thad's feet never touched the ground. He was so thrilled. He loved to play and was delighted to know he was going to have another sibling to play with. Once Austin was born, Thad would come in the house frequently to check on the baby then run back out to play.

Thad sang to me even before Austin was born in his sweet sing-song voice, "He's my baby, he's not your baby!"

We were a normal family with three children. Noel's parents lived across the street from us, so we even had extended family close by.

Our home was a popular place for games—a favorite was Capture the Flag. We played different sports according to the seasons: whiffle ball, kick the can, and roller hockey. Everyone loved playing football in the fall. Rollerblading on the school parking lot was a favorite, with Ryan leading the charge and making sure to include the younger children who looked up to him.

Men and women coming home from work joined in. We played outside every night with the neighborhood adults and kids. Everyone enjoyed it. I am glad to have these happy memories. There is a bonding that happens when adults and children play together—happy and laughing as summer shadows make their way down the sides of the houses and the cicadas sing.

FEARS CREEP IN

A few years after we were married we were at the movies when we got the call that Noel's younger brother Dirk, fresh out of rehab, had flipped his car. He also was young and handsome. He was a little brother to me, and I was very close to him. He had so much potential that would not be realized. The attraction of alcohol to Dirk, like the famed apple of the garden of Eden, was too strong and its temptation was ultimately fatal.

I had fears of my children dying as they grew up. Does every mother? I had a dream one night while on a ski vacation with three other couples. In the dream Ryan died. When I awakened I was in the lousiest mood. *What an awful dream! Why would I dream that?* It was scary. As the day went on I began to forget. Still, I took the opportunity to tell Noel we needed to pray more together as a family, and especially to pray *over* our family. I felt an urgency that we needed to be protected spiritually.

BONES OF CONTENTION

After another son was born there were many times I desperately wanted Noel to fill in the gap when I had reached the end of my patience with the kids. I needed that tag-team partnership. I had longed for support, but it never seemed to happen. Communication between us always seemed to be difficult.

I admit that I constantly hounded Noel with "We gotta pray for the kids, for our marriage!" I never felt satisfied that it was enough. Noel had a real heart for prayer for people, especially people outside of our home, and he was gifted in this area.

There were times though when I felt an extra sense of urgency to pray for our *own* children. I knew I could pray on my own, and I did, but I also knew that Noel's prayers as the spiritual head of our family would be the most powerful and effective in covering us with protection and blessings.

I once took a class about spiritual gifts and learned that I had the gift of mercy. That class put my parenting strengths and weaknesses in a whole new light. I was able to see how my gift of mercy came into play in my parenting. I began to see that my specific gifting in life made me the person I am, and others' gifts made them the people they are. No one gift is better than another. They are all a part of the whole when viewed in the light of the spiritual gifts in the body of Christ.

One thing I learned is that people with the gift of mercy have a tough time parenting because they are likely to be merciful to their children in many situations instead of allowing the child to experience the natural consequences of their behavior. This was apparent in my interaction with my kids. When they didn't agree with a consequence I gave them, I felt bad for them. And I'd wonder if I needed to back down on the decision I had made. Admittedly there were times when I did back down and lessen the severity of the punishment. I think this confused the kids.

One time Ryan came home after his curfew. I was supposed to take the car away. I took it away for awhile but gave it back to him earlier than I should have because I was the one being inconvenienced. I didn't do a lot of things right.

I didn't necessarily sit down and explain things to my children when they were little. I took for granted what I thought to be obvious, and I see now that wasn't the best way.

When Austin was about two a friend came over for a visit. Austin got very jealous and started behaving badly. I got down on his level and said, "I like our time together, Austin. I love you. But it's also fun for me to have a friend come over. She's going to stay for a little while. You can stay here too. Or you can go off and play. Then when she goes home we can have our time together." Surprisingly, he understood and responded in a rational way. At two years old! Of course it doesn't always happen that way. Kids are unpredictable. There are times when they simply don't understand.

When Noel and I tried to talk about our different parenting styles, blame would always be placed by one or the other of us. It didn't seem like we got anywhere.

I remember going to my parents' house for Christmas after Ryan died. On the drive I asked Noel, "What are you thinking?"

"You don't want to know what I'm thinking," he answered.

I had no idea what he meant. But I knew I was sad and without hope because we were simply unable to have a conversation about our pain. I felt so alone because he was unable to communicate with me. And I wasn't able to communicate with him.

Ultimately, after Ryan's death our marriage succumbed to defeat. After Noel and I divorced I realized that maybe we didn't have the tools to make our marriage work. I had to accept responsibility for my own shortcomings. Possibly they were catalysts that led us on the path to divorce.

Being a stay-at-home mom before Ryan died was a hard job. I put a lot of effort into trying to enhance the lives of my children and make a comfortable home for my family. Afterward I became a working woman, and it seemed like it wasn't possible to put that much time into my family and do all the daily tasks to keep a home running. My life was turned totally upside down. Things felt daunting. Feelings of inadequacy because I was divorced hounded me. *I should have been able to keep my family together. I, I, I. Me, me, me.* How would we make ends meet? I identified with the widow Zarephath from the scriptures whose oil didn't run out even though it wasn't physically possible. I knew, even in the midst of this painful divorce, I was being taken care of.

I always worried about how the boys would react. They never talked about it, though once they came to me and expressed their worry about me.

Thad was hurting but never verbally blamed me. "I never thought you and Dad would get a divorce" was the only thing he ever said. This was hard for me to hear. Even though I knew this was the right decision, it caused my children great conflict. I felt like their mental and physical wellbeing depended on my decision. Yet that very decision was hurting them.

I remember talking to Thad and Austin when they were about twelve years old and eighteen years old and telling them I was praying for them to be best friends. It was painful for me to watch them fight or not like each other. It was torture to see that they didn't have the closeness they used to have when Austin was small.

Both boys looked at me with incredulity and laughter. I insisted I was going to pray and believe that it would happen. We all walked away without agreeing. I decided I had no control over their relationship, and I turned the issue over to God.

Chapter Five

RYAN

Welcome to the Under Town
Where things just seem to flow
There is no such thing as control for yourself
Down in the Under Town
Things fly by
Right past your naked eye
Down in the Under Town
Your life is controlled
Your soul stoled
Down in the Under Town
Where you stay to be buried in the Under Ground

-Ryan
1997

When Ryan was small, strangers stopped us in the store to comment about the darling boy with the red hair. One man stopped us to touch that red hair. He told me there was something special about this toddler with the beautiful blue eyes.

What does one say when a three-year-old child comes to you and says, "I wish I was in Heaven"? When he was a little older he said he didn't think he would live a very long life. He was simply making a statement. There was no fear present. I sensed that it was an awareness he had and he wanted to let me know something that he knew. He was honoring me by giving me this knowledge. I listened and tried to understand. If I asked a question the potential was that Ryan would shut the conversation down. That is what happened.

Ryan was seven and a half years old when his cousin Jonny committed suicide at the age of eighteen. Later Ryan commented, "God will use these circumstances for good." A very mature quote for such a little guy.

When Ryan and Thad were little, Noel built an addition on our house. Ryan used the loft above the addition as his bedroom when Austin came along. The only problem for me was that it was separate from the rest of the family—like he had his own little house. I never wanted him to be that far away from the rest of us.

Ryan spent a great deal of time working by his dad's side on woodworking projects. At an early age, with Noel watching carefully, he taught Ryan to use the band saw. It was clear he had superior hand-eye coordination for a boy eight years old. He also showed great concentration and determination to use these skills to make things. The neighbors often saw him coming down the street with a wagon load of his newest hand-created items to sell.

SELF ESTEEM BOOSTS

I wrote monthly journals as Ryan grew—cute quips he made or positive qualities I saw in him. The purpose in writing was so that Ryan would see his value. I felt he could benefit from positive written words. Here are a couple of those journal entries:

March 1991 – Ryan age 10
Ryan is such a loving person. "Mom I just love Austin so much," he said. "I think he is so cute. Why don't we have another baby?"

Ryan has been getting all of his spelling right on his tests this month. He worked really hard to get them all correct. Ryan won an award for third place in a "Goal Shooting" contest this month. He also won two trophies for the best looking car at the Pinewood Derby races in Boys' Brigade.

Around his tenth birthday Ryan made some comments that indicated his self esteem was low. So we planned a sleepover with several boys. I felt he needed to hear some positive things about himself from his friends. I made a poster and all of the guests were asked to write one thing they liked about their friend Ryan. I had each boy bring something that was characteristic of them to bury in a time capsule in our back yard. The plan was that we would dig it up on Ryan's eighteenth birthday.

Cody brought a plastic Ninja Turtle toy that said "Cowabunga!" Ryan put in a golf ball and tee because he loved to play golf. Thad put in several small toys. We dug a hole in the backyard—a dream come true for a pack of ten-year-old boys. We buried the time capsule. I will share more about this event in Chapter 8.

TEENAGE YEARS

Ryan was gifted in many ways. When he was twelve or thirteen he tried to explain that when he looked at certain objects he heard various types of music. It seemed his visual interpretation of the world around him could open up a whole new world of understanding inside his head. Where others saw only a leaf or a blade of grass, Ryan heard certain sounds. That was his brain's way of interpreting things.

Neither Noel nor I had any musical knowledge, so I didn't really know what to make of what he said. When I watched the movie *August Rush* I wondered if Ryan saw things through music the way the boy in the movie did.

Maybe this gift was his way of learning. Some people see colors when they have different feelings.

Was this bothersome to Ryan? I wonder that too. There were so many times when I asked him a question about how he was feeling or how he understood things. When he tried to explain, it was like he hit a wall. He could only articulate so much. Then he would quiet down, not really saying much after further questioning. This lack of ability to verbally convey his feelings really frustrated him.

November 1992 – Ryan age 12
Ryan announced that he got to play first chair trombone
one day at band practice. He especially liked playing
the solo part. He is gifted in playing musical instruments.
(I say that because in the last six months, he's only
practiced his trombone 2 ½ hours or less!)

Ryan communicated well through the written word. He was a good writer. I looked through the tests that he took at the beginning of ninth grade. The psychologist said he had a moderately high level of intelligence, but verbalizing what he wanted to say got mixed up a little bit in his head before it came out.

My oldest son could always stand on his own. One day he and his friends built a ramp in the street so they could do rollerblading tricks. There was a woman in the neighborhood who often yelled about things she didn't like. And this time she called the police to report the boys. The policemen came and asked the kids not to skate in the street. Once they left, Ryan marched right up to this neighbor lady's door and asked her why she had called the police. I think she was more than a little surprised, as everyone else was afraid of her. It was astonishing that she didn't yell at Ryan.

Ryan went along with most everything, but sometimes he just plain marched to his own drummer. One time he played his harmonica instead of his trombone in the high school band class. He played all the right notes—just on the wrong instrument. He couldn't believe the instructor couldn't hear the harmonica sounds. He only got into trouble when the instructor actually saw him playing it. The band instructor didn't think it was funny, but other band members sure did. Every time I think of Ryan doing this it makes me smile.

Another "marching to his own drum" event happened when as a youth Ryan went to wilderness camp. When he came home he shared that he had kept the same piece of gum in his mouth throughout the whole week. He even slept with it in his mouth at night. I don't know what that accomplished except that he could, and he did.

Ryan loved playing baseball and made many good friends through those sports experiences. He was employed at an after school, part-time job by a local craftsman who made ornate wooden boxes from exotic woods. He was good working with his hands.

In the winter months our family made our way to the frozen ponds to speed skate on ice. The older boys enjoyed racing with other kids, and their cousins often raced against them. Ryan enjoyed skating on the ice and also with inline skates. He was a good skater.

Snowboarding was another sport Ryan enjoyed very much. We have wonderful memories, pictures, and videos of our family on Colorado vacations.

A whole new genre opened up for Ryan when we

purchased a video camera. He and his best friend Cody put their creativity to use making funny films. The films varied from Mission Impossible themes to a take-off of MacGyver. My personal favorite was Illiterate Rainbow—a spoof on Reading Rainbow. Looking back now at the themes he chose for his videos, I see a pattern working its way through the stories—someone dies in many of them.

Ryan was part of an amazing youth group where he was active in leading worship music at various times. There were many opportunities to participate in musicals the group performed for the church. Ryan loved being involved and often added his own touch of humor to the mix. He was well-liked and respected.

I asked him once, "Can you tell a difference between your friends at church and your friends at school?" He answered that there was no comparison. He felt very loved by the friends he had at church.

One youth group sponsor commented that Ryan was a very important part of his small group and instrumental in helping other youth grow in their faith. Noel and Ryan went together with the church group to Mexico the summer of '96 (the summer before he robbed the bank) to help build homes for families in need of housing. The pictures they brought back from the trip were of a Ryan who was full of joy! He was very happy to be helping other people.

If asked to describe Ryan I would say what a sweet person he was. Without reservation I would say he was a responsible, respectful, kind, considerate, and loving son, brother and friend. My relationship with Ryan was precious. When he was a teenager we had a fun way of sending each other messages, left written in code on the refrigerator—a fun way to stay connected as he expanded in the world unfolding before him.

RYAN'S STRONG WILL

If Ryan didn't want to conform he would try very hard to have things happen the way he wanted. For example, he hated wearing the shirt for Boys' Brigade, an elementary aged boys group at church. He claimed it wasn't comfortable. The dilemma was that the boys got points for wearing the shirt to their meetings.

"You can wear the shirt and get the points," I said, "or you can not wear the shirt and not get the points. It's that simple. I'm not going to force you to do either one."

His Brigade leader, however, thought I should make him conform.

Ryan was extremely strong-willed. I had to choose to give him consequences when he exerted that will. I tried to pick my battles, not fighting over unimportant things.

When Ryan died the police report said how many times he was shot. Some people were outraged about that, but the police said that when he went down he picked his gun up and pointed it at them again. I wouldn't believe that of any of my other children, but I did believe it of Ryan. He was capable of doing something like that, being fully responsible for what he was about to do and the consequences of it.

FRESHMAN LETTER TO SENIOR SELF

In a note from Mrs. Danforth, Ryan's Freshman English teacher, she said, "When the class of '98 were freshman, they wrote letters to their senior selves. I would love for you to have Ryan's. I was so saddened by his untimely death. That quiet redhead with the cute smile who sat in my freshman language arts class will always be in my memory. That's the Ryan I knew and will remember."

Hello my future self. How are you? I'm sure this sounds real corny now to you but oh well! Hope you can still read your own writing. I hope that you (me) have done your best in school and better still, have at least a higher GPA than a 3.5. Hopefully you have a car and a good $ job. You better be keeping active in some sport or something. Your best friend better still be Cody. You better be a 10x stronger Christian now than you were as a freshman. You better witness a lot and you better be a better person.
You deserve to die if Kelly is not your girl friend any more!!! You better always be faithful to her and be the best guy you can be. I hope you are a great musician by now. Maybe a good piano player and a great guitar player. Your family life better be real strong and hope you've kept a great attitude about everything. Hope you still love snowboarding. Well, that's all I have to say, future self. Except have a great life. Best of luck

From,
Freshman Forever Ryan

P.S. You better not grow up and become mature. Be a kid. Be yourself and hey, you're cool and yes, the sun shines on you 24 hours a day. .

LEARNING DISABILITY

During the summer of 1996 Ryan had some testing done to help with school work. The doctor's comments included: visuoperceptual abilities very superior at 99th percentile. Mental arithmetic quite good." Reading and spelling, however, fell into the 16th and 8th percentile indicating a severe developmental learning disability. Ryan didn't qualify for help with those disabilities at school because of his high IQ—superior range

92nd percentile. He was encouraged to go on to college. But because of this learning disability he felt frustrated. I believe he fell between the cracks in a school that helped students excel at the high end of the scale and at the low end.

Ryan didn't want to be singled out and ask for longer time taking tests because of his reading comprehension. I didn't feel it was my place to intervene for him. When he was without hope of getting help he began shutting me out, and began to find a solution that he thought would work best for him. He and I had many discussions about his difficulty concentrating in school. He started coming home for lunch and I noticed he seemed happier. When I mentioned that he appeared to have found a way to break up his day at school and make it more tolerable, he didn't answer me. He gave me a look like *he wouldn't comment because I wouldn't understand.*

After Ryan's death, my sister found Everclear hidden above his closet. Everclear is a liquor that doesn't give off much odor. I wondered if he had been coming home during his lunch hour to self-medicate as his means of coping.

I got a tender, caring letter from an anonymous person. "Lately Ryan has fallen away from God. And has gotten into a bad crowd. The scariest part is that he has supposedly been doing heroin. We never have witnessed him doing this, but a trusted friend has told us this." These friends were concerned for his safety.

When I asked him about heroin use, he denied it convincingly. But he told a friend that his drug use was harming his relationship with his family. He quit using all on his own and started to change his attitude. After Ryan died his freshman girlfriend Kelly shared with us that Ryan was really upset that she and several other friends had written us the letter about their suspicions that Ryan was using drugs.

In retrospect, I believe Ryan began drinking and using other substances. They were having a negative affect on his mental and spiritual health. On the outside he tried to keep the same persona. On the inside he indicated through his writings that he was not pleased with himself.

We were thankful to learn after Ryan's autopsy that there was no alcohol or drugs in his system.

TRAIN ROBBERY WITH IMPLICATIONS

One year at the Old Thresher's Reunion in Mt. Pleasant, Iowa, our family rode a train around the property. During the ride the train was robbed by young men wearing bandannas over their faces. The men had fake guns and fake money. They reenacted the robbery while interjecting comedy—that way it wasn't scary to the children, but funny. We all laughed as the "bad guys" passed out candy to the kids. After one bad guy was gunned down, he lay in the street. When the lawman had his back turned he would come back to life, sit up slightly, and hand more candy to the kids. Then amid chuckles from the audience he would lie back down and play dead. Today this harmless reenactment looks too much like what actually happened in Ryan's life.

MEMORIES FROM AUSTIN

"Ryan looked out for me," said Austin. "He and Thad teased me and picked on me, but I loved it. When Thad picked on me, Ryan jumped in and played the role of my protector. I guess it was kind of self-righteous of me, but I loved it. Ryan was cool. He was good at everything and he did all the cool things I knew of—skateboarding, rollerblading, made his own videos, photography, wore cool clothes, snowboarding, playing guitar, had a girlfriend, and he was just happy. That is how I remember him.

"When as a family we rollerbladed in downtown Cedar Rapids, Ryan jumped around and did crazy stuff. He launched off curbs, and one time he landed right next to me. His spirit just towered over me."

LAST MONTHS

In the last months of Ryan's life I began to see a lack of desire in him. He didn't want to go snowboarding, one of his favorite sports. He seemed depressed but declared he wasn't. We had many conversations on this topic which all ended with Ryan denying he needed help. I stepped things up a bit and took him to his pediatrician. Ryan convinced both his doctor and the intern that he was not depressed.

FROM RYAN'S JOURNAL – June 1996

*I realize I am so lucky, all I have is so great. I just
NEED to keep asking what I can do to give back? What
can I do to help?*

*When you wake up in the morning, look at the clock
and realize the time from last time is gone, it will never
return. When you wake up dead and realize that you took
advantage of the time that was there the time is gone now.
It's like the A Train that you know is coming. You just have*

to wait for it before it's gone.

*What is the point of this for now it's gone?
Your Mama tucks you into bed but when you wake up
your mama's gone. It's like the day when it turns to
night it doesn't come back.*

In another journal entry in June of 1996, Ryan wrote:

*Life is great. Leah gave me a letter and I got it today.
That was awesome. Time goes too fast, you never
have any time to do everything.*

BELIEF IN GOD QUESTIONED

The last year of Ryan's life he sometimes said he didn't believe in God. He didn't share the conflict he was feeling as a Christian. I didn't expect him to be perfect in his walk with Christ, so I didn't know that he felt the need to have his life so aligned with God. It sounds like it was tearing him apart. Was it a normal struggle teenagers face? Mental confusion? Or spiritual warfare?

Right now my religion means nothing to me. Why?
Because God hasn't impacted my life at all. He's never
"talked" to me or done anything for me, at least that is
noticeable, and for weeks the only thing I have done with
God is pray that if he is real he will show me. Well,
where is he then if He's real, sleeping? Well, until he
makes a noticeable difference on me, See ya.
Journal entry, June 1996

Ryan was confused and went back and forth on his feelings about God and faith. He seemed to have turned his back on God and instead pursued his own means of happiness, feeling even more separated from the One who created him. His friend Kelly shared in a conversation in January 1997 that Ryan had told her "he had a plan that was 'bigger' than living for the Lord." When she asked him what it was he refused to tell her.

Ultimately, I know Ryan was a Christian and that he was forgiven for his sins. I had heard him pray and ask Jesus to forgive him of his sins and be the Lord of his life. He is with God in Heaven now.

When I think back on what I would have wanted for Ryan's life, it's the normal things. Senior homework, prom, last-minute college applications. I wanted Ryan to get married and live a fulfilled life according to the gifts he had been given, maybe even have children.

I always wondered if God was calling Ryan to be a pastor or a preacher or a musician. I will never know. On the other hand, I might already have the answer because of what his story has become, what God has taught me through my son's death.

Ryan was not a pastor or preacher in the classic sense. There were no seminary studies. No ordination. He was, however, an avid learner of all life had to teach him. Perhaps all of those things he pondered and secreted away in his journal were the things that were meant to be there for us to learn from.

FROM RYAN'S JOURNAL – JUNE 1996

*Sometimes people are gone from our lives in the blink
of an eye in the midst of a thought. Sometimes we never get
to say goodbye. But what is a goodbye? In saying goodbye
there are no right words no wrong words. Only memories are
goodbye for without them goodbyes are nothing. Not
enough words could be said, not enough emotions could be
expressed in a goodbye. There is nothing but memories.
Goodbyes are not good – or bad but something to deal with
in life. You must go on after your goodbyes for they are
nothing more than something to get over in life, something
to deal with, and most of all something to cherish. Goodbyes could be a single word or they could be a life time of
memories.*
They are what you make them.

Chapter Six

POSTHUMOUS DISCOVERIES

When things are gone
they are always there in our memory.
No matter how long or how far they are gone
they are still there in our memories.
If we make it that way.

Ryan's journal entry

I've heard it said many times "hind sight is 20/20". When I thought about the days and months surrounding Ryan's death, I remembered many things. Perhaps if they had happened in close proximity to one another it might have made a difference, made an impact that could have changed the course of history. But they didn't. They happened over periods of time and in no specific order.

Looking back, I realize that when I began searching for Ryan on that fateful day it was just the start of a nineteen-year search for finding out what Ryan wanted us to know. Thoughts and memories are shared here in hopes that something might be helpful to you, the reader.

For a long time it seemed like I was the only person who actually knew and believed that our sixteen-year-old son could actually follow through with a final act of suicide. We had such a close connection. I have never personally known a person who possessed as strong a will as Ryan had. I knew he had the tenacity and stubbornness to decide what he was going to do, plan it all thoroughly, and do it.

On the last day of Ryan's life when he came home from school and asked me to go to lunch with him, I felt a force that let me know I wasn't even supposed to turn and look at him or engage with him. My own son. I felt like someone was protecting me from interacting with him in those mundane moments.

It was so strange when I think about it all these years later. I never looked upon Ryan's face that afternoon. The last time I saw his face was when he left for school that morning.

In hindsight I would say that what played out that day was supposed to play out. It is the ultimate letting go when you realize that nothing you could have done would have changed the trajectory of a day that would change the rest of your life.

I beat myself up for years before realizing this, of course.

The note that Ryan left for me that day which said "Mom went to Kyle. I will probably eat over with him 2" had the picture on the side that looked like a clown with a hole in his head. It makes sense to me now. I think that hole in the head was a bullet piercing his forehead. Maybe he was even thinking of himself as the clown. He *knew* what was going to happen.

I've long heard that other people have premonitions of a loved ones' passing. Even the person who dies sometimes has thoughts about his impending death.

Noel coming home from his UPS delivery route in the middle of the day was out of the norm. And bringing little animals home was also unusual. I distinctly remember thinking, My husband doesn't come home in the middle of the work day bringing baby bunnies. Looking back, I realize Ryan had probably already been killed, and I think Noel may have known something had changed.

SYMBOL OF DEATH

The first bunny died a few hours after Noel's rescue. I believe its passing was a lesson for Austin to see first-hand the natural process from life to death. We tried desperately to help the second bunny cling to life and create a distraction from the heaviness that filled our home on that long evening. All our efforts failed, and when we returned home after burying Ryan we found the bunny had perished. It was a finality in the nightmare we had just lived through. Austin and I laid the little fellow to rest in the backyard with a funeral of his own.

Another sign—Ryan's friend Kyle called to ask if Ryan was home on the day he was missing. I knew this kid well, and that day his voice was altogether different from his normal voice. This call was another validation that something was terribly wrong.

RYAN'S CONCERN ABOUT HIS BROTHER

One of Ryan's biggest concerns as a teenager was his brother Austin. Austin struggled when transitioning to different activities throughout his day. His anxiety during those times affected the family, as well.

Just weeks before Ryan died he took me in another room while Austin was having a meltdown. "You have to do something about him or he is gonna be a criminal!" Ryan said adamantly.

"What are you talking about?" I responded. "Your brother can probably hear you! Be careful what you say!" I was angry with Ryan for saying this within earshot of Austin. But I never got a deeper explanation about his meaning.

Was Ryan thinking about ending his life as a criminal? And he didn't want Austin to follow in his footsteps? He certainly recognized that Austin had a lot of emotional stress, and he seemed to be fearful for his little brother's future.

Ryan had such a heart and concern for his brother. I believe he knew his plans, and I think even then he wondered how the aftermath of his decision would affect both of his brothers. As messed up as his thinking was at this point in time, he still thought so much about the people around him and how they were feeling. He was sensitive to everything and everybody.

THE SKI JACKET

That last morning when Ryan left for school he was wearing my Lands' End ski jacket. The next day when friends started to gather at our house after we had identified Ryan's body, I remember opening the coat closet and seeing that jacket hanging on the farthest side, away from the rest of the coats.

I have to say here, Ryan *never* hung his coat up. For sure he never hung it in the hall closet. I picked it up, and in that moment grief overwhelmed me. I had a decision to make. Deny my grief so others would be spared hearing my cries? Or be true to myself and let myself grieve fully?

I started bawling. I held the jacket to my face. It smelled of his shampoo and cologne. Those small memories—you never want to lose them. I am certain Ryan left the coat there for me to find. It was the first time I felt like Ryan had a deeper message that he wanted to leave behind for the rest of us.

Finding that jacket was a turning point for me. It made me realize I needed to fully grieve so that I could heal. It was also the first time since his death that I felt a deep connection with Ryan, as though he was saying to me, "Don't be afraid to go deeper here, Mom. You can do this."

OTHER WAYS OF BEING READY

Ryan often told me I needed more pictures of him—another way he tried to take care of us before he died. On a vacation in

Colorado the winter before Ryan died he often asked to be videotaped. It is clear now that he wanted us to have all the video of him that we could possibly have. Nearly everything we did on that vacation as a family was documented.

UNUSUAL MAIL-ORDER PURCHASE

One day about three months before he died Ryan said, "Mom, I want to place an order for some stuff from this magazine." This particular magazine had an array of gadgets. Ryan told me he wanted to purchase some tools used for opening locks, so I assumed he wanted to buy something for one of his woodworking projects. He was sixteen and I wanted to be respectful. I didn't have any reason *not* to trust him.

When he was on the phone with a representative from the company, he handed the phone to me. The guy on the phone said, "Ma'am, are you okay with your son placing this order?"

I didn't ask, "What did he order?" And he didn't say, "He's ordered a starter pistol." Ryan had told me the order was for tools, and I believed him. No parent wants to believe their child is going to pick someone's lock illegally. No parent wants to believe their child is ordering a fake gun to rob a bank.

Afterward we found out Ryan had ordered the starter pistol, a gun that only shoots blanks and is used to start races. This is the gun he took into the bank.

Before Ryan died, Noel was busy outside. He found something in the garbage and brought it in the house.

"What is that?" I asked. "What could that be from?"

It was a metal case with a place for bullets in the top. There were two bullets missing. These were the blanks for the starter pistol.

Thinking about this situation later, I wondered why you would need blanks if you were just going to make the bank teller believe you have a gun. I believe now it was Ryan's plan to fire the blank, forcing the police officer's hand if he hadn't already shot him—that this event was not so much about robbing a bank but about being killed. Having thrown the remainder of the blanks away, I had to assume he wouldn't need the gun again.

LATE AND I'M IN A PANIC

Several months before Ryan died he was invited by his youth sponsor to attend The Salt Company, a weekly gathering of Christians from Iowa State in Ames, IA. I felt comfortable as they left that evening, but as the hours crept towards midnight and he still wasn't home, panic began to set in.

I thought maybe Javin, Ryan's friend, would have stopped to use a pay phone to say they were going to be late. He didn't. I woke Noel up, frantic. It was about two o'clock in the morning when Ryan came in. His youth sponsor just dropped him off. I grabbed Ryan. I hugged him tightly. I sobbed. I hung on to him for dear life. He didn't know what to do.

I have always wondered about that night. Were the events of that evening supposed to happen that way so Ryan would know how much I would miss him? Was it my chance to grieve with him while he was still alive? I kept bawling. Noel and Ryan were both shocked by my intense crying. It was so unlike me. All Noel could say was, "See what you did to your mother?"

The whole scene strikes me as funny now. Noel didn't know what to say. Ryan was shocked. He just let me hold him. We must have been quite a sight.

I do know that my firstborn prepared himself for his death. In a short conversation a month before his death Ryan tried to convince me he wasn't a "needed" family member. My words did not seem to reassure him of his value in our family. He was dearly loved by all of us, so I was at a loss to understand why he thought that.

Ryan cleaned up relationships with friends and relatives both physically and emotionally.

During spring break he stayed a week with his best friend Cody and told him jokingly that when he died he wanted his hand positioned in a "hang ten", where his thumb and pinky finger were sticking out and the rest were folded into his palm. We don't think, however, that Cody knew anything about Ryan planning to rob a bank.

Ryan's girlfriend Leah, on the other hand, said later that he joked about robbing a bank. He had kept his family from getting to know Leah better. A few weeks before he died, Ryan wanted to break up with her. I can see his reasoning. If anything happened to him, he didn't want it to hurt her so much. Yet he left flowers in her car on the day he wrote his "Goodbye" poem.

I noticed that he never seemed to invite all of his friends over at the same time. He made sure nobody knew the whole story or got together long enough to be able to figure out his plans.

Ryan went over to Kyle's house a few weeks before he died so Kyle could take pictures of him. Ryan was really into photography and all kinds of arts. He was so creative! Kyle took silly pictures of Ryan standing by the garbage can, lying on his side with thumbs pointing up at the camera, and modeling gloves.

Kyle knew Ryan was planning to rob the bank that last day. I don't believe, though, that Kyle knew Ryan had the starter pistol or that he had a plan to die.

It took many months for Kyle to tell us that a day or two before the robbery he had asked Ryan, "What are you going to do if you get caught?"

Ryan responded, "Let them shoot me."

Three months before he died we celebrated his cousin Jake's birthday. While Ryan, as an older teenager, didn't always want to do things with his family, he went peacefully to Shakey's Pizza on that evening. There was something purposeful about him being there. I could tell something was different, him spending time with family. Many times during that evening he looked at me, knowing I sensed something.

Another time, Ryan was determined to spend time with my mom and me. My parents came over for dinner and we played darts. It seemed as though he made a conscious effort to spend time with us—all part of his plan for us to remember, *When I'm gone they will have had this time with me.*

When I asked Ryan if he was going to be in the school's talent show about a month before he died he said, "I hope not." I didn't know what to make of that comment at the time, but of course later it made sense.

HAPPINESS COMES

Ryan suddenly became happy. Light. Fervently present in each moment.

One happy sign was when Ryan enlisted Thad and Austin to fill up water balloons one Saturday. They went up to the top window of our house and threw them down on their dad when he came home. They had so much fun. This hadn't happened in such a long time. I loved the air of playfulness that had entered our house again. But something in the back of my mind said, Maybe this isn't so good. Was I seeing the "too-happy" calm before the storm?

Because of Noel's nephew's suicide, I had done some reading and studying on the topic. I remembered that one sign of an impending suicide was sudden happiness. All of a sudden a person's mood changes. His depression appears to have resolved itself. Family members think he might be okay, but the only reason he is happy is because he sees a way out of the pain. He makes a decision to end his life.

I even shared with Noel what I had learned—that people who are thinking of committing suicide can be depressed for months and then all of a sudden appear happy and carefree because they have decided what they are going to do. From what I had read, family members give a sigh of relief and think everything is okay. They think the sufferer has turned around and is getting better. Noel agreed, but he didn't know what to do with the information any more than I did.

GOING TO CALIFORNIA

Ryan talked often the winter and spring before he died about going to California to learn how to surf. Neither Noel nor I were encouraging a road trip to California. Ryan was too young for that kind of trip. He liked the movie *Point Break* about a bunch of bank-robbing surfers. At the end of the movie the bank robber ends his life by diving into the surf.

I believe that "going to California" became a euphemism for saying his life was going to end—like someone else might say "hang up my cue stick" or "cash in my chips."

Noel, however, said, "I don't believe it was suicide. I believe Ryan was planning to buy a car with the robbery money and go to California." He thinks Ryan only wanted to die after he was caught, and he commented that if he was in the same position he would rather be dead than alive too.

HUMOR TO BE FOUND

Even in the midst of all of these posthumous discoveries, there were moments that I think are funny now but definitely were not at the time.

One afternoon a few months after Ryan's death we overheard Austin talking to Kyle.

"So Kyle, I heard you drove Ryan to the bank."

A tense moment, to be sure, as Thad and I were in the room too.

Austin gave Kyle a really intense look and said, "What's the matter Kyle, are you feeling a little guilty? " He nodded his little head accusingly, as though agreeing with himself.

This was extremely confusing for me because on one hand I felt bad for Austin. He was seven years old and trying to process what had happened to his brother. On the other hand, I wanted to give mercy to Kyle and help him feel better.

No one over the age of seven had any idea what to say.

Another time Austin approached me and said, "Why didn't you teach him not to rob a bank?" That struck me as funny because in Austin's little mind we should have taught Ryan not to do these things and then he wouldn't have. It was all so logical, simple and endearing.

POLICEMAN'S THOUGHTS
& MEMORIES

The Cowboy

I watch the Cowboy as he rides around,
with his head high,
some say he rides in style,
but the only style he has is what others give to him,

but he rides,
gathering up a herd that is now his own,
he owns the herd,
he controls the herd,
which they do not realize,

he does what he wants with them,
not realizing how he can hurt,
and how he can kill,
for the herd does not realize,
that it's all a game,
a deadly game,

he seems to do only what he pleases, the only thing in his way,
is the land,
which he rides on,
as he pleases,

-Ryan
1-17-97

*I*t's with me every day from the minute I wake up to the time I go to sleep. Everyone expects the police to be all-seeing, all-knowing, above reproach," Troy said. "A high standard should very well be placed on those of us who have sworn to keep citizens safe and uphold the law. That said though, we too are human. We go into situations with very little information and mere seconds to make life and death decisions. It's a humbling profession."

Troy remembers the day Ryan was killed this way:

"My partner was driving the car that afternoon. We had the 3 to 11 p.m. shift. At 3:30 we left the station. We were on the way to my house to pick up my raincoat and happened to be driving down Old Marion Road when we got the call.

"I remember looking to the right and seeing the bank the dispatcher described. When the dispatcher said the name I immediately said, "That's not the right bank." But it had recently changed its name, so at this point we weren't completely sure that it was the correct bank.

"My partner made a fast left-hand turn, signaled oncoming traffic to stop, turned on his emergency lights, and drove into the main entrance to the bank—eleven hundred block of Old Marion Road. A woman at the drive-through window was on the phone. I thought she must have been on the phone with my dispatcher. I couldn't think of another call so important that you would be on the phone during a bank robbery.

"Both my partner and I thought for a moment she might be a mannequin. Her face was white as a ghost. Her eyes were so big! Her face registered that something was going on there. She was pointing behind her.

"Our mindset was to drive around the bank slowly. About ten seconds later the suspect came running out the front door. I wasn't driving the car so I had no control over where our car was going, and I was frustrated by that. My partner got things situated so that he was driving right alongside the bank robber who is running about two feet from my car door. My partner tried to maneuver that huge car so that we could be as close as possible to the suspect so we could grab him.

"By this time he was right alongside the passenger window, where I was. He was still running and our car was keeping up with him. I had the passenger-side door open about halfway, and I was about one second from jumping out and grabbing him.

"This is the moment that kills me. This is the moment I have played and played and replayed again for over seventeen years of my life. This is the moment when he turned and I caught sight of a gun barrel right in front of my face. I didn't have time to do anything. I didn't have control of the car—I was just along for the ride that day.

"Instinct kicked in. I fired the gun in my right hand. I think one of the shots hit him in the hip. Even injured, he ran a few more paces still pointing his gun at me.

"The car stopped. Sirens wailed. The glass in the passenger-door window was broken. Shattered. I remember that the suspect had fallen to the ground. As I got out of the car and went over to apprehend him, he raised his head, and incredibly he pointed the gun at me again.

"My gun went off again and it was over."

CONFUSION REIGNS

"Everything was so confusing. The suspect had a bag of money in his hand. Purple smoke billowed from the bag after the smoke bomb went off, making it more confusing and disorienting—not just to the suspected robber, but to the police as well.

"I remember standing over this person afterwards—this person who I thought was trying to kill me. I didn't know what he had done in the bank or how terrorized or terrified those people were. I remember trying to do something for him as he lay on the ground. My partner, who was also a paramedic, said to me gently, 'No, Troy. There's nothing we can do for him.'

"'Shit, Pete,' I said. 'I just killed somebody.'

"The gun was still in his hand when he died. With one hand I flipped the gun out of his hand, a couple of feet away from him. I remember thinking that it looked like a .380 caliber.

"It was raining. Glass was everywhere. I was directed to go back and sit in the car. I was shaking like a leaf, and I couldn't see out of my right eye because it had glass in it.

"An ambulance arrived and a paramedic, a woman whose kindness and whose name I will remember forever, put her arms around me. I'm no mama's boy, but for a few brief minutes, I felt safe and everything was okay."

DAYS PASS

"A couple of days later I found out the gun was a replica .380. It was a huge blow—just kicked me right in the head.

"Another day or two later I found out it was a

sixteen-year-old boy. Another blow! Like somebody took a two-by-four and hit me across the face. It just kept getting worse. If it had been some guy who was strung out on drugs or if he had a long criminal history it would have been more bearable. But he was a boy! With a fake gun! That was horrifying to get past.

"From the time the police got the call to the time it was all over was less than 36 seconds. There was not a whole lot of time for reflection then. That was a lot to occur in 36 seconds."

DWELLING ON THE MEMORIES

"I still don't know how my partner drove the car the direction Ryan was running. In all the chaos and confusion I wondered how a big bulky Chevy in such a confined area was able to keep up with him. We cut him off. He made a right hand turn, then crossed the street again. The shooting happened in the middle of the street. I have taken the situation and turned it all around in my head. I still can't figure out how he crossed in front of the car to the passenger side. It's like he knew that I would be more able to engage with him than the driver would.

"If Ryan wanted to die, he did it right. He knew how to do it. I don't know how the situation could have been anything other than a suicide. His face was covered with a ski mask. He seemed confident, like he knew how this was going to end. He was doing everything he could to make it end this way. He placed himself in such a way as to give me no other option but to shoot.

"I remember telling people at the time or shortly thereafter, 'I wish he would have shot me.' I wanted to get shot.

"After many hours at the police station on the night of April 30 I was allowed to go home. No one came with me. I didn't have any family in town. After the incident, there was no sleep for a couple of days.

"My supervisors asked if I wanted to be reassigned to a different area of town. I was told I could take psychological leave because of this incident and my part in it. I have a strong work ethic and I told myself, I'm not going to let this divert me so greatly that I let it beat me. I wanted to keep doing my job. I don't like to be seen as weak.

"I don't hate anybody. I'm not angry at anyone else about what happened that day. It's just the circumstances I hate. I don't hate Ryan for doing this, for whatever reason he thought he needed to do it. He was at the age where you're usually thinking about college. So much to look forward to. I couldn't know what was going through his head that day. But I do think, what a waste. What a waste of a person, a beautiful life.

"I still do think about the 'what-ifs'. What if it hadn't been raining that day? What if my partner had taken the interstate that day to get to my house to pick up my raincoat? My partner later asked me, 'Troy, if you were driving that day would you have taken the interstate to your house?' I think he was going through the 'what-ifs' too.

"I wish my mind would forget what my eyes have seen."

HATED WORDS

"A big thing that really, really bothered me was that people didn't know me. And they didn't know Ryan. They knew nothing about the situation, yet they weighed in on the incident. Suddenly people became armchair experts on what happened, why and who was at fault. People did not know the extenuating circumstances. They went with their guesses.

"Even the guys I worked with were trying to make me feel better by saying that I did a good job. Still, it made me so mad to hear that. I didn't want anybody to say, 'I guess that's what he gets.' They didn't do what I did and someone did not die because of it. It was not their finger that pulled the trigger that ended a young boy's life. So many people minimized it. I did not want pats on the back for doing what I had done in that situation. I didn't want to hear, 'Great job.' There is no good in this at all. Everybody loses. Unless you're in my shoes, you can't know that it was never that simple.

"In recent years there have been many stories about police officers killing young men. Everyone acts as though they know exactly what happened. Even the media. Everyone believes they have enough information with which to make an appropriate judgment call. I feel for everyone involved in those situations—the person who was shot, the cop, the families of both. I know because I have been there. I've lived it.

"People within the police department knew within a short amount of time that I didn't want to talk about this. I wanted to be ignored. In the long run, it was a sixteen-year-old kid with a replica gun. That's what it always came back to."

DEALING

"In the months afterward, the whole scenario didn't seem like it would be a big deal to anyone else. But it was in the front of my mind every waking minute. I felt as though I was wearing a mask with a happy face on it. I was so depressed, in such a gloomy state.

"I had killed a sixteen-year-old kid. I looked normal on the outside, but in my mind it was a way to function. Inside it was tearing me up. I was afraid to look in the mirror, thinking I would see this horrible monster. I felt low and dirty. I completely lost my innocence.

"Before April 30 I was seeing a counselor because of some issues in another police incident. Many times I thought about committing suicide. The thing that kept me from pulling the trigger was the thought of my mom grieving over me. It would have been like giving up, and I don't want to give up. I never really quit anything. But I admit, I felt desperate during those months following Ryan's suicide.

"I'm sure it would have been better if I had had someone close to me, but I didn't. I lived alone—no girlfriend, no wife, and no family in town. I had the worst possible thing—other cops. They patted me on the back. There wasn't a thing I could do to show them how much I hurt. I wished I had their naivete."

THE PARENTS

"Years later I was able to meet with Ryan's parents. Their response to me after I shot their son in the line of duty was so compassionate. They forgave me. To this day it just blows me away. They lost their boy—their child—yet they didn't have any animosity toward me. It's really remarkable.

"There are many good people like them who have been through horrible things and who also have no animosity. Even in the most rotten, negative situations they still hold their head up. They get the facts, they're able to look at the situation logically, and though this is the worst hurt in their life they are still understanding.

"I always assumed the parents had every bit of information. Everything. But they didn't know I was within half of a second of jumping out of the car to tackle their son. Just a half second and things could have been different. I have replayed that scene so many times in my mind, wishing I had jumped sooner. Or Ryan had flashed that gun half a second later. It helps me to know that Dawn and Noel can see things now a bit from my perspective.

"Dawn and Noel have faith. They're bulletproof. They have a shield. It is unbelievable. They have always looked at the big picture. They know there's something better waiting for us after this life. I respect anyone who is so strong in their faith. They're the best people in the world. No matter what happens they still have their faith.

"Noel and Dawn divorced after Ryan died. I thought they divorced because of this incident. It makes me feel a little bit better knowing that what happened on that day wasn't the sole reason for their marriage ending. I've never cried about anything except this. Ever. Even when my dad died I didn't cry.

"My life changed too. I married and my wife has been a springboard for me, a shoulder to cry on. We have a strong marriage, but she has suffered alongside of me—my mood swings, anger, and erratic behavior. She's a very good person. To know her is to love her."

MY REASONS FOR SERVING

"I wanted to get into law enforcement because I love fighting for the underdog. There's a certain satisfaction about laying your head on the pillow at night knowing you helped someone escape a dangerous situation. Or just a talk while you drive across town in the police cruiser with a kid in the back seat who hasn't had a father figure in his life.

"As a police officer I have one philosophy: I work for you. No matter what. I don't care who you are. If you're a convict who's given us problems in the past, I'm going to work to a conclusion based on your current actions with me. The police department is there for regular everyday people—the average citizen.

"The incident with Ryan has honestly made me a better person. Whatever it is that I'm dealing with on any given day, I think to myself, 'It's not as bad as what happened on April 30, 1997.' Even if everyone isn't happy, at the end of the day everyone is still alive.'"

"When I retire someday I want to write a billboard that says, "Thank you, citizens of Cedar Rapids. It's been a pleasure. Wonderful people live in this town." Wonderful people, people who believe you had the best intentions in your work as a police officer. People who trust that all you want to do is serve and defend the public."

Chapter Eight

GRIEVING

He thinks it's easy
To say goodbye.
He isn't around
To hear me cry.
He planned it all;
thought it wisely through.
He could not discern
what I would do.
He wanted it easy
for me to say goodbye,
He left in April and
I'm still stuck at "Why?"
He knew I'd be carried
by the Lord so true,
He didn't know that day
a part of me died, too.
Au Revoir, my son.
Love, Mom
7-11-97

You think you're going to talk to your loved one again when they get home from school or when you get home from the grocery store or that night at dinner. When that next talk never comes—and it never will this side of Heaven—that's a very hard thing to take. It's a very difficult thing to process. And it takes time.

I agonized over the fact that my son wanted to see me one more time the day he died and I essentially said, "No, I can't go with you because my hair's more important." I didn't say it that way, of course, but as his mother it made me feel awful. I hated my hair for awhile after that. The cut was fine, but what it represented in my mind was me letting him down.

In retrospect I often contemplated what our conversation would have been like that day had we gone to lunch together. For years I thought I could have talked him out of his foolish act. Then I realized I may have been protected in some way I can't explain.

Then I learned to let it go.

When Ryan died, a part of me died too. That part remained dead for years. The only way to describe the pain aptly is to say that I wasn't sure my lungs would even remember how to draw the next breath of air.

My friend Marilyn gave me a magnet with this important message on it: "My grace is sufficient for you." (from II Corinthians 12:9) I looked at that magnet regularly and prayed, "Lord, just get me through this day . . . this hour." I was so filled with pain. I felt a hollowness that only a mother who has lost a child can explain. Still I always prayed because I trusted God.

My greatest desire was that God would make something beautiful from this mess.

God had other plans, though, and brought to me a capacity for more joy, fullness, and purpose in living than I had ever known before. But that process took a long time.

No matter who you are and no matter what you're going through, God can take the shambles of a broken life and create something of immense beauty and value. All He asks from us is our trust.

In those years after Ryan's death I did my best to parent Thad and Austin. My memory seemed nonexistent. My energy level was so low. Grief is like trying to run through chest-deep water when everyone around you is cruising along normally. No one can understand why you just can't keep up. Parenting while grieving is even more confusing.

The first few months I was still in shock. But then the terrible sting set in, and I wondered how the rest of the world can go on when my heart was so utterly shattered. I began to notice other people who had lost children at various ages. I encouraged myself by focusing on the fact that they survived the loss. Grief is so hard and it takes so much energy. Sometimes just breathing was the best I could do. The end of each day felt like a small accomplishment.

A BUDDY INDEED

In December, nine months after Ryan died, I knew it would be difficult to celebrate Christmas without him. I wanted to surprise the family. I began to pray for the perfect dog to join our family. A gentle, calm dog who wasn't "yappy." I looked for a grown dog that was fully house-trained but wasn't able to find one.

I responded to an ad in the newspaper for a Cocker Spaniel puppy. A gentleman was also there, deep in the process of puppy selection.

"How do you pick just one?" I asked the owner. "You don't," he replied. "Don't you know, they pick you?"

The little buff-colored male the other "puppy customer" had been holding leaped from his arms and made his way to my lap. He never left my lap during my entire visit. I knew then that I had been chosen. The puppies in the litter were not ready to leave their mother, so arrangements were made for me to pick up our puppy a few days before Christmas.

We needed a name for this little guy. The second-grade class at Austin's school saw the puppy at Show and Tell and tried to help us pick a name. One girl raised her hand and offered, "You should call him Blender because his tail never stops moving in a circle." Thad suggested calling him Rambo, and it got serious consideration. Ultimately we named him Buddy and all were satisfied.

There was something special about this dog. No one mentioned the sense of pervasive peace that his presence provided for our family. I think it could only be described as a deep knowing presence that in some small way (but certainly big to us) Buddy connected to our dearly beloved son and brother. This gave us peace and healing in our grief. We all loved Buddy and he loved us all right back. He was the answer to my prayer for a quiet, relaxed dog.

When I think about Buddy these years later I cry tears of grateful joy. God had gone above and beyond what I had asked Him. He helped us find a special dog that had the gift of loving us unconditionally in the middle of our lives' deepest hurt. We all grieved Ryan in our own ways, but Buddy made us feel that sometimes just enjoying the sweet love of a dog was going to be enough.

When Noel and I divorced, Buddy was fifteen months old. He came to live with Thad, Austin and me where he faithfully provided a quiet stability in our home.

Through the latter years of Buddy's life, the Lord provided a lot of healing for us. It is intriguing to note that the end of Buddy's life was monumental in the healing of Austin's and my relationship. Here is how it happened: I had become very fearful that the death of Buddy would cause additional hurt to my sons who were both young adults by this time. I had been doing a lot of alternative health care for Buddy to help him enjoy a longer life.

I talked to Thad about letting Buddy go and he was supportive, saying that he didn't want Buddy to suffer. It was several months later before I was able to talk to Austin about ending Buddy's suffering. When I did, Austin was also supportive and helpful during the entire process.

So what was I afraid of?

I asked myself this question and suddenly the light bulb turned on. *Dawn, you can stop trying to control Austin's life by keeping the dog alive. The two are not connected.* Suddenly my own attempts at making sure my boys were safe came back to stare me in the face. I confessed this to Austin and realized that my relationship with him had come full circle. By trying to control Buddy's life span for the boys' sake, I'd just simply not been respecting them. This was a healing moment in both Austin's and my life. I came to realize that I never had been, wasn't now, and never would be in ultimate charge of Austin's fate.

Before Buddy died, Austin brought him an edible card to chew on. I was proud that he was able to spend time with Buddy and talk about his feelings, something everyone in our family had trouble with.

The time came to say goodbye to our beautiful Buddy. Austin held him as life left his body. Buddy came to our home for a purpose, and now that purpose had been fulfilled. He was a blessing to all of us.

CELEBRATING RYAN'S 18TH BIRTHDAY

Previously in Chapter 5 I described Ryan's tenth birthday party and how his friends brought things that we could put in a time capsule to be opened on his eighteenth birthday. Ryan died though, four days before his seventeenth birthday.

I had always envisioned the mostly eighteen-year-old birthday party friends standing in our yard as Ryan dug up the time capsule. I wanted to invite them to join me on May 4, 1998, but I was concerned about the pain they would feel with that activity. Maybe I couldn't bear looking at their faces and dealing with their grief on that day.

When his birthday came around I had another problem. I despaired over not being able to remember the location of the buried treasure.

I prayed fervently for several days. Then I ventured out to the backyard. I started digging under the farthest walnut tree. I dug a few holes and then realized I couldn't dig up the entire yard just to find this capsule. I reached a low point. I felt without hope. I begged God to let me find this capsule so I'd have this extra way of remembering the boy I'd lost. I just couldn't lose the time capsule too.

Suddenly the thought came to my mind: *If you were to bury it today, where would you bury it?*

I instantly perked up, knowing the thought did not come from me. I scrambled over to "Ryan's Tree," a walnut named for the simple fact that as a young boy Ryan swung for hours from a ski rope and handle attached to the lowest tree limb. I stood in the exact spot where I thought I would have buried it at that moment. I prayed one last time, "Lord, please let me put the shovel in the exact spot where it is buried." I was too exhausted to continue much longer.

I put the shovel a few inches into the ground and felt it hit something. The plastic bag. I continued an inner monologue and thought, That looks like something I would have put the time capsule in. And it was! I had wrapped it in several plastic bags to keep the rain out for all those years. I hadn't buried it more than a few inches deep, because I wanted to be able to find it easily. However, I recognized that I never would have found it on my own.

I was thrilled and am still touched over God's grace in answering my prayer. Finding the time capsule felt like an embrace from Him.

I relayed the story of finding the time capsule to each boy—about my answered prayer and the thrill of knowing God cares enough about us to help us find even a box full of toys buried in the back yard. It was sad not having Ryan there to see it, but it gave me a joy deep down in my soul that is hard to express. It was a healing moment to be able to give back to the boys each item placed in the time capsule eight years earlier.

Looking back, I'm not sure it was my idea in the first place to bury the capsule. Ryan was an amazing kid. I felt then and know now that God had a purpose for some of the things like this that occurred during his lifetime. Things beyond our control were being put together for a grander purpose. I believe that purpose might have been God showing me how much He loves me. I also think God wants me to tell Ryan's story to bring glory to Himself. I see God's hand weaving the different parts of Ryan's life into this story.

SHARING YOUR GRIEF WITH CHILDREN

Somewhere along my healing journey I learned that while you are grieving you are supposed to tell the children who are around that you are grieving and that it has nothing to do with them. They are not the cause of your grief.

Children are naturally self-centered so will automatically hold the false belief that they are responsible for the negative aspects of what we are going through. They are watching us. They are watching our reactions, seeing how we deal with trau-matic events.

Instead of leaving them to silently guess what is going on, they need to be told exactly what is happening and how to respond in an age-appropriate way. When we don't give them those tools, we leave them flailing in the dark. It's not fair to them, and as a result many children are traumatized by events they don't understand.

Here's an example. My sister's friend died of a heart attack. We all went over to see her when we found out. Her son brought his daughter, who was about three. What does a three-year-old think when she sees her grandmother crying and the adults in the room trying to comfort her?

I got down on her level and said, "Grandma is sad, but it isn't because of anything you did."

No one thinks to explain these potentially confusing life events to a child. I voiced this aloud to Adryan and watched her walk right over to explain it to her mother.

Kids tend to think, *Should I have done something different? Did I do something wrong? Is that why we're here?* They can think all kinds of things, and those untrue things can follow them right into adulthood, causing them to believe untrue things all their lives.

Part of my healing process has been to let go of the things I didn't do exactly right.

MESSAGE TO PARENTS WHO HAVE LOST A CHILD TO SUICIDE: YOU TOO WILL SURVIVE & THRIVE

To a parent whose child has taken his own life: there is hope. You won't always feel at the edge of a deep hole, wondering if the slightest breeze will blow you in. The pain can get better and ease with time. There is hope for you to make it through this. But the only way to be done with grief is to face it head-on and walk through it. You will feel the most excruciating pain you've ever felt for awhile. When you're fresh in your grief, all you can think about is today.

One day you will be able to breathe in and not feel a stabbing pain right below your heart. You will no longer dread every birthday and holiday. Maybe you'll even start to find solace in those days instead of pain. It can happen, and it will happen if you are open to it.

Today probably feels like the horrible end to a formerly beautiful and promising future. I know. I've been there. You will laugh again. The tears will slowly stop. Your future will look different, but your life's tapestry can be mended by a God who promises to wipe away every tear from our eyes.

When we are faced with trying to help someone who is grieving we want to catapult them out of their pain. We want to make the pain go away. The really healthy thing though—and the only thing that will make a lasting difference—is to join them where they are today. Trying to get someone out of their pain is akin to trying to remove a tooth as it is growing in.

I felt like I got the chance to start to heal when people in my life just let me be where I was in my grief. They didn't press their own expectations of where I should be on to me. There were friends and family who didn't try to propel me forward or hold me back. They just let me BE.

1997 GOODBYE LETTER TO RYAN

To My Dearest Ryan,

I am writing this letter to say goodbye to you. I don't want to say goodbye but I don't feel like I have a choice. I miss you so much. I don't have anyone to go rollerblading with. I loved our times of joking together. I loved it that you always cared about what I thought. You are very precious, and I have lost a wonderful friend. I didn't know my worst nightmare could ever happen to me. It is torture being in limbo. I'm angry that you think I can do this, miss you like I do, and go on. I'm so scared that I'll forget things about you that I want to hang on to. You were so dear to me. And to lose you is devastating. No one can ever take your place. The pain I feel over losing you is the worst I've ever felt.

I'd like to think that if you had time to think about leaving, you would have chosen to stay because of the pain others would feel. Then I remember the conversations we had throughout your life. When you were little I can remember you telling me you wish

*you hadn't been born. When you began adolescence you commented
that you didn't think you'd live a very long life. When we first
discussed finding a college, you told me you felt like you'd have to
rob a bank to pay for college. Then there were the times you said
that you would like to be in the Mafia or be a modern day Robin Hood.
I tried so hard to get you to tell me more. You only shared the minimum.*

*I feel like I did something wrong because you wouldn't share
your hurts and secrets with me. I will always hurt when I think about
you. I have some wonderful memories of our relationship together.
I am so thankful for them; you are a fantastic person. Why did you
HAVE to do it, Ryan? Couldn't you have said to yourself, "This is
wrong! I can't do it!"? Were you so miserable that you just didn't
care about anything?*

*Why wouldn't you let us get help for you? Do you still
think you can do all things yourself? I am letting you go because I
know you are in the best place ever. When I come there you'd
better be prepared for a never ending hug. I love you dearly.*

Mom

I suppose it's a cliche to say that when a child dies, not only do
you not have the child, but your dreams for them die too.
When Ryan died in 1997 there was no more Ryan present physically, but the future had already swallowed him up as well.

But I have two living sons. My prayers for them moving
forward are now spiritual in nature. Before Ryan died they were
just as much (or more) physical: Keep them safe and out of
harm's way and make them happy. I want what God wants for
them. To live the life God has purposed for them. I can't
pretend to know what that life looks like. Whereas before I may
have tried to push what I thought was best on them, today I
want God's work in their life to be fulfilled. I wish for them
deep and abiding peace and joy.

I hope that parts of this story give my two sons wings to fly. I hope they feel it in their hearts. They have such kind, gentle hearts. It always has been and still is such a joy to watch them interact with the world around them. I look forward to watching them in their future relationships. I think my expectations of them are much less because I realize I don't have control over their lives.

That is freedom.

Chapter Nine

MOVING PAST GRIEF AND INTO LIFE

Little By Little

I once thought
that my only link to you
was my grief.
I couldn't let go.
I knew if I did
I would lose us both.
But one day when I couldn't
take the pain anymore,
I decided to try.
So slowly and carefully
I let go of my death line to you,
and I was surprised to find myself
being held by God.
Little by Little,
step by step,
I learned that I didn't need
to hang on to the death
to remember the life.
What a joyous discovery!

Kittie Brown McGowin
Montgomery, AL

Four or five years after Ryan died I realized his not being physically here did not mean I wasn't still fundamentally connected to him. Our love for each other still transcended the gap of grief. Once I read the poem at the beginning of this chapter, I realized I didn't need to hang on to the pain of Ryan's death to appreciate the beauty of his life. It totally changed the way I thought and how I felt. I knew Ryan already had the best of everything in Heaven. He didn't need me forever making amends or continuously longing for him. He already had the perfect ability to forgive and to love.

I used to be afraid of losing the memories I had of Ryan. I was afraid I wouldn't remember how his cologne smelled on him, or how his hair looked when different lights shone on it. It was the feeling of losing even more of him in small increments—the initial loss and then the gradual loss of my memories.

PROFESSIONAL HELP

My heart felt like a bicycle-sized tire had run over it and left it divided in two. The tire tread mark left it permanently indented.

I worked for Dr. Michael Goad, a chiropractor, for several years. He used various types of alternative therapies to help his patients. A few years after Ryan's death Dr. Goad tried a therapy to help my body heal from the trauma. During this treatment I was able to remember what Ryan looked like with more clarity. His face came closer and closer to me and went into my heart. And the tire tread came out. Just like that. It was amazing and so healing. I felt Ryan's presence nearer all the time after this experience. I didn't have to look at his picture or say anything. He just existed. I carried him in my heart after that. We still had love for one another. Nothing took that away. It was a gift then and still is.

Several years later Dr. Goad began using a therapy called

Quantum Neuro Reset Therapy (QNRT). This therapy helps unlock painful memories from the brain that are associated with traumatic events. Some people hold on to negative emotions attached to events that have happened in their past. Our bodies constantly react to them when presented with a physical stimulus that reminds our body, and subsequently our mind, of the original trauma.

I found the biggest progress in this therapy when I read God's Word and prayed. I asked God to help me make the connections between my body, mind, and spirit. He helped me in a major way through QNRT therapy. The person I was before and the person I became after were vastly different. I could see my situation and my life from the point of view of an outsider looking in. I could look at it objectively. I could see the past hurts and pains for what they were and let them go.

I would not be able to tell this story without Dr. Goad's work with me. He is a wonderful, godly man who serves God wholeheartedly. He has mentored me throughout our friendship. Without his dedication to helping people in situations like mine, Ryan's and my story might still be stuck somewhere inside me, unable to be told because of the immense pain I was in. My body would not have allowed my mind to reprocess all of that information in a healthy way.

While this therapy worked very well for me, others might decide to go with more traditional medicine or counseling. It's important that each person find what works for them.

HEALING IN STEPS

I also found a 12-step group that helped me to understand how to deal with difficult issues in life. As I studied the steps I began to take responsibility for my own actions and slowly found freedom from the guilt that weighed me down. I finally figured out that I wasn't in control of my kids' destinies. I realized that

I was not in charge of their present, their future, or even their memories of the past. Ultimately they are the holders and keepers of their own future. That was a hard lesson to learn in the wake of Ryan's death. I wasn't ready to learn it right away. It took years. Looking back, I realize that's okay.

The defenses I had as a mother to keep the bad things away were mostly these: 1) fearing some imagined negative outcome occurring in one of my children's lives, and 2) my doing, saying, or thinking something that I thought would protect my children.

The entire 12-step process is designed to bring one closer to a "Higher Power." I personally "let go of my own perceived power" and let the God who created me take control of my life in a greater way. With God's help, I've gotten rid of that constant sense of shame I learned to take on as a young child.

By getting rid of the guilt and shame in a healthy way rather than covering them up, I had a higher capacity for God's love. I had so much more room to be filled up. I then had so much more to give.

One of the most important things I am learning along this journey is to love others one hundred percent of the time. When I concentrate on loving others with more intention, it leaves less room for fear. And it leaves fewer opportunities to manipulate and try to control situations that make me feel uncomfortable.

I used to think I had to be perfect and that my kids did too. Now I know I'm definitely not going to be perfect on this side of Heaven and neither are they.

GRIEF WORK

One thing that was confusing to me in the wake of Ryan's death was the conflict and confusion of being angry with him and grieving him at the same time.

Once I understood Ryan had planned his death, I was able

to find a support group for suicide survivors. Some people feel shame and guilt connected with suicide. The loved ones remaining don't think they should get help or that they don't deserve it. Many people feel like the suicide of the loved one was their fault. Sometimes family members won't admit that the death *really was* suicide, so they don't want to rock the boat.

I still felt a huge portion of this tragedy was something that a "good" parent should have been able to help their child avoid. It helped to read the stories Ryan's classmates wrote about him. I heard what people said about regrets over not knowing what Ryan was going to do. I thought, they are all feeling like they should have done something. It wasn't just me! It was a whole community of friends, grandparents, siblings, teachers, everyone hurting.

They all thought they should have known something, seen something—that a small part of it was their fault. There's an extra layer of grief to deal with. Suddenly it fell over me—a veil of absolution cloaked my shoulders in peace. So many people thought it was *their fault,* and it couldn't have been everyone's fault.

The grief group I joined was a very small group—one other person, the facilitator, and me. Being with this group on a regular basis took a lot of courage, and it was very helpful. I felt understood. I was no longer alone in my grief experience.

THE CALL TO SPEAK OUT

I knew God had something He wanted me to do, and I was perfectly happy to wait until He guided me right to it. I was scared to think he wanted me to talk in front of a crowd. But I had peace knowing that God would never take me to a place where He had not given me the tools I needed. At the same time, I was very happy God was not saying I had to tell the story right at that moment.

It's a good thing too, because I was still trusting in my own abilities. I was encouraged to know that this God who loves me so much would somehow support me with the growth He was going to make happen in me. I knew that I would get in the way of God telling this story. He would have to take me out of the picture, so to speak. All He needed was my willingness. I felt like a little girl placing my hand in His so He could lead me to full maturity.

I never once told God I wasn't ready. It was something fully known between us. I always trusted He would guide me to where I am currently.

Wow! What a journey!

RECURRING DREAM

The dream is always the same.

It first came to me in the midst of a fitful sleep a few months after Ryan died. Here's the gist of the dream:

I am at the Ellis Park ice rink, the same park my father took me to when I was a little girl. The park held grand memories for me. At the ice rink there are high banks around the pond. There is a little hill to walk up to get to the warming house. There used to be a shack there where a person announced the races, his voice ringing out in the crisp winter air. Excitement at the ice rink was electric! Lots of people came to cheer the racers.

In the dream I am an adult. I am speed skating around the rink, then slowly going through my cool-down routine. My dad is still on the ice in his boots, but almost everyone else is off the ice. The meet is over.

Everyone looks toward me. They're waiting for me to make a speech of some sort. They are looking toward the announcer's shack, but now there is only a cement pad there. I am called by a higher power to walk up the hill toward that concrete pad. I realize I am supposed to put the guards back on my skates so the blades won't be dulled. It is not easy to walk up the snow-covered hill in the skates.

If in my dream I realized the walk up that hill will take nineteen years, I'm not sure I'd have started out in the first place. It's a walk filled with tears, anger, confusion, sorrow, and hope. My feet will surely grow tired along this treacherous journey.

There's a microphone at the front of the concrete pad once I reach the summit. Everyone on the shore is watching me.

In my head my small, scared voice speaks to God. "I don't have any shoes to wear."

My head turns and my eyes settle on Ryan's shoes. I know I will somehow be able to do what God is asking of me when I take my skates off and put on those shoes. Somehow they are a physical manifestation of that higher power encouraging me to find my voice.

There they sit, inviting me.

I see this dream being fulfilled as I write and as I prepare to speak about this time in my life.

My journey thus far has been about healing, grace, and mercy. But it has also been about recognizing truth. I could always intellectually know what God says about me. But some part of me wasn't able to let it be fully true. Ryan too was unable to believe the truth about himself. So many people are deceived.

I reached a place where I could think, Wow! It really feels good not to care what other people say or think about me. I have always been sensitive. I wanted everyone to like me and say what a good person I was. I still struggle with those things to some extent, but I recognize them for what they are now. I wasn't able to distinguish those thoughts as lies before. I am learning to believe what God says about me and not what other people say.

I'm sixty years old and I've made really great strides in

knowing who I am in Christ. I've come leaps and bounds in my identity. That has allowed me a freedom in knowing that no matter what happens I will be okay. So many people still have trouble understanding how I can be so at peace with how Ryan's life ended and the many twists and turns my own life has taken.

My desire is to help others heal. When I said yes to God about writing this book, or at least beginning the process, I knew He was going to help other people to heal. Maybe that person is you. Perhaps you have lost a child in a similar manner.

Or maybe it is you who are thinking about ending your own life because you think you've run out of options.

Maybe you're the father whose prodigal son has not come home.

Or maybe you're the sibling who watches as your sister or brother slides down the abyss into alcoholism or drug use.

God is so much greater than our current affliction. He taught me all of this along the way. I can say it because I have lived it. I have chosen the clothes my sixteen-year-old son would wear in his casket. I have looked into the devastated eyes of my seven- and thirteen-year-old sons who were just sure they were the reason their brother was gone. I have wept as I signed divorce papers. I have struggled to breathe.

When I look back on my life and see the relationships I chose with people, it's a blessing to see how God directed them.

Everyone can be used by God. Thinking you are not a part of a greater, amazing story is an absolute prison. You're not meant to live like that. There is NOTHING in your life that cannot be redeemed by God. NOTHING! Please, please don't believe the pernicious lie that there is.

No one deserves forgiveness. It is a gift. All we have to do is receive it from the One who created us. "Because of the

Lord's great love we are not consumed; for His compassions never fail. They are new every morning." Lamentations 3:22-23a

What I have learned in joining this community of suffering is that there is beauty here, but only for those brave enough to learn how to see it. For many years I was not brave. I was too scared of what I would find when I came before God with my brokenness and pain, with the hurt and disappointment of trying to make sense of what I had hoped the future would be versus its reality.

I was stripped of so many things I always thought would be there: Ryan, my husband, friends who moved away.

All of these things happened, and I was unable to see that nothing in my life apart from God was going to heal me. I could not control the outcome of the lives of those I loved, no matter how hard I tried. God wanted me fully trusting Him.

I had spent my childhood and my whole adult life trying to hide my shortcomings. I didn't think people would accept me. The event of my son's suicide cracked open my shiny veneer. All of the things I had tried to keep hidden were finally exposed. I was broken and only God could heal my broken heart.

JULY 2014 LETTER TO RYAN

Dear Ryan,

It has been awhile since I've written to you. A lot has happened. Dad and I divorced in 2000. It was so hard on all of us to go through the divorce. There was so much pain.

Dad and I didn't have the skills we needed to make it through the difficult times. A few years before you died I remember praying to God about what to do about my marriage. Do I stay or leave? I asked God, "What should I do?" I heard or knew in my head that God said,

"Something is going to happen that will make it easier to decide." I said, "Okay, but I don't want to know what that "something" is."

I left that topic there with God that day. Then when you died I prayed in agony over whether or not to stay in our marriage. That was not an easy decision to make. Both boys were struggling and needed help. I wanted to get help for them but Dad said it wasn't necessary.

Thad struggled through his teenage years, but is now a wonderful, loving man. Both of your brothers have a great relationship with Noel now. Dad and I have both remarried. I am working with Rachel Swanson-Hillestad to write your story. God is directing the process.

I miss you so much! I can't wait to see you again. We had so many great times together. You were such an awesome son. I took great delight in being your mom. Thanks for all the memories. They fill me with joy... until we meet again . . .

JULY 2016

I read Ryan's "Goodbye" poem again. It's funny how it means something different to me nineteen years later.

I pondered what he was thinking when he wrote it. Before, I looked through the lens of how I felt about it. The lens was clouded with anger and fear. I didn't want him to say goodbye. Or I wanted it to be a misunderstanding. Now I see through the lens of the mother who is further along in the stages of grief, and I see that he was most definitely saying goodbye. I believe now that I knew he was saying goodbye, but in the ensuing years I accepted this fact with more serenity and grace.

I have spent lots of time thinking about what Ryan's goodbye poem said and what I've learned since then. Thad and Austin have taught me too. Be thankful for the day that you have. Don't think too far into the future, because there can be so much imagined worry and trouble there. Or even real worry and trouble. What is it going to help to worry about all of that when you could be happy and alive today?

Chapter Ten

LIFE RENEWED

Come,
take heart,
Find Healing,
Live again--
Love again--
Maybe even
more
than you
did before.

J J Young C.S.P.

The short poem above was on a little bookmark that was tucked into a sympathy card we received in the spring of 1997. The poem is special to me because it was sent to us by Troy, the policeman whose gun took Ryan's life. I discovered it while writing the book. I am very happy to say Troy's kind words written that day and this poem have come true.

It's been so many years, and now I've spent a lot of time thinking about my kids who are living. I enjoy each day with them. I am so thankful for all I have.

A NEW CAREER

A few months after my son's death I became a student at Capri College of Massage Therapy in Cedar Rapids. I chose this career path because it gave me a means to use the gifts God had given me. Another important factor in my decision to become a massage therapist was the fact that I was able to work for myself and choose my own hours. I could see clients while the kids were in school and be home with them before and after school.

Because I had been living with chronic pain for many years, I had discovered Neuromuscular Therapy (NMT) to be helpful in giving me pain relief. After I earned my license for Massage Therapy in 1998 I continued my education by pursuing my certification in NMT—a very specific therapy for working with people who suffer from injury or chronic pain. I have maintained my own practice since then, and at different times I have supplemented my income by working for various clinics and chiropractors.

The most recent modality I have learned in detail is Cranial Sacral Therapy (CST). This modality is a very light touch therapy that helps the autonomic nervous system to balance itself. CST is branching out to pioneer some amazing results working with people with brain disorders, Alzheimer's, and chronic fatigue syndrome to name a few areas. If interested, you can learn more by going to https://www.upledger.com.

I look back at the "life experiences" I have been through, and I see how the culmination of my experiences are used in my practice to help other people. I am so grateful for the clients God has sent me over the past nineteen years. I find joy in helping them gain better health and pain relief. They all hold a special place in my heart.

ADDRESSING MY OWN LONELINESS

About a year after our divorce I was finally able to talk to God about my loneliness. I asked Him to bring someone into my life with whom I could do active things. I missed having someone to bike with or play tennis with, someone who enjoyed all those things as much as I did. Many people understand first-hand that it's not only the spouse and family who are torn apart in a divorce. You also lose friends.

I joined a women's racquetball league at the Rockwell Recreation Center where I was already doing massage therapy a couple days each week. Unfortunately, the league was canceled. One other woman who had joined talked me into moving to one of the men's leagues—the "C" league. I played one game. Embarrassed at my skill level, I left a phone message that I was dropping out.

Several days later I received a phone call from a gentleman in the league saying I had missed our scheduled game. I explained that I had dropped out of the league because I felt inadequate.

Do you notice this recurring theme in my life—fear of appearing inadequate?

This man talked me into setting up an alternative game date and assured me he only wanted a chance to play, the same as I wanted. He did not care how my racquetball skills added up.

I definitely didn't want to disappoint him by standing him up again, so I went. The game went okay and I had fun. The gentleman encouraged me. I decided to stay in the "C" league since they had not received my message about dropping out.

When I arrived the next week to play my match, a different guy was hitting balls inside the court. A woman stood outside the court watching. I assumed they were a couple and she was checking out his skills.

When I walked into the court this thought popped into my mind: *Is this the man I'm supposed to meet?* It was never a thought previously on my mind.

Just like that, it was the beginning of our relationship. Brad took my phone number. He knew of another woman who might be interested in playing racquetball with me to help my game along.

After that, however, we found ourselves spending more and more time together. We got along great and found lots of sports we enjoyed. We joined other people speed skating on the indoor ice rink in Cedar Rapids. The last time I skated outdoors was before Ryan died. I often wondered about the dream God gave me to come off the ice to speak. Why was I at the Lou Dennis Rink at Ellis Park when God spoke to me?

I know the outdoor ice rink after a speed skating meet was my place of being grounded and safe with my dad's presence nearby. The nervous tension and the pressure of competition was behind me. I found a place of "peace"—just like where He has brought me so I could tell my story. I am in awe of how God led me to this understanding.

In the summer Brad and I in-line skate on the trails. We've done several marathons and made lots of friends over the last several years.

Time with Brad is fun and comfortable. He is laid back, gentle in spirit, and slow to speak. The most amazing thing is that Brad accepted me and my feelings. With his help, I learned to express feelings that had been buried deep inside me. I quickly learned he would not reject me for stating the way I felt. In fact, this led me to feel safe in growing in my faith again.

Brad and I dated for several years, then married in 2009. I felt different about myself when we married. I felt more complete and acceptable to others. I don't know if it was this way in reality, but it's the way I felt.

THAD'S WEDDING

Thad married a wonderful woman in 2013. He chose his brother Austin to be his best man. Following is Austin's speech:

"Despite all the pink bellies, wet willies, whatever kids do to each other—today you know
I love you. I'm so glad you honor me with this
privilege. It's an honor to be here and be
sitting at your side. Thank you for making me
your best man. I really appreciate it."

Thad stands up and hugs Austin. With arms around each other,
Austin continues to talk.

"We grew up in a family with three brothers,
and it's no secret that we lost one. The reason
I think today is so beautiful is because it's
about gain. To me, it marks a new moment
in our family because it's like a new
beginning. It's really great to see the
blessings that God has given us. Our
family is expanding and thriving now.
I'm really excited to see what the future
holds."

The two of them do a funny brother rap about future children,
and everyone in attendance claps and cheers.

As I watch them I'm remembering the prayers I prayed for
them when they were eighteen and twelve—that they would be
best friends.

Austin's "best man" speech delighted me. To see them
communicate with each other and to know they have a good
relationship with each other and with their father was very grat-
ifying. Having Austin acknowledge Ryan with all of our family
and friends present seemed to fill up the last empty space left
in my heart by Ryan's absence.

Many people came up to me at Thad's wedding. Some
were Thad's friends, people who walked with him through

those difficult days after losing Ryan. Some were in-laws whom I had lost in the divorce. They were all kind and loving in their attitude toward me. Sharing those bonds of love, even though Noel's and my marriage union no longer existed, was affirming and healing.

I felt like everything came full circle that day. I had prayed faithfully for God to heal our family through all of our hardships and pain. I had trusted in His promises to restore the years that the locusts had eaten. (Joel 2:25.)

Several of Thad's friends spoke to me during the reception, giving me great encouragement.

"You are a beautiful woman. You have done a great job with your kids."

It was special that they would take the time to say encouraging words to me. It was a happy time of looking back and seeing all God had done.

ICING ON THE CAKE

Seeing Austin marry a wonderful woman in 2015 has also brought great joy. Since I gave him back to God and relinquished trying to control his life I have learned a great deal. The experience of witnessing his wedding brought peace to my soul. God can do amazing wonders when we don't put Him and His children in a box.

I have gained three daughters-in-law, the third through Brad's son who married a few months before Thad did. I adore each one of them and am thankful to have women in the family.

The greatest adventure began in May 2016 when I became a grandmother. Thad and his wife brought a bouncing baby boy into the world. I have watched him grow for only a few months, and I have pondered the comments of grandparents before me. All of their observations are true. When I see the love my son and his wife have for their baby, it warms my heart. I am doubly blessed to feel my own love for this little boy. What satisfaction. I am taking in all these wonderful changes as they come, appreciating what I am given. I am not promised I will have them tomorrow. So I will enjoy them today.

SEEING THE CHANGES

In those early days after Ryan's death I sat at his grave and cried. My dreams and my world shattered. I wished for the ground to swallow me up.

I rarely have days now when I remember something about Ryan and cry. My nervous system has been healed from much of the trauma associated with Ryan's death. With all of the work I did with Dr. Goad, I'm able to remember the good times I had with Ryan and look forward to seeing him again one day. I am no longer filled with the crushing despair.

I blamed myself for a lot of things concerning Ryan. Letting them go helped me. Healing takes time. It's so gradual that sometimes you wonder if it's even taking place—or if you're getting anywhere at all. Then one day you realize you are better. That you're able to do some small thing that a few months ago you wouldn't have been able to do.

Now I listen to people's comments after someone dies. I think, Why couldn't I have thought that or understood that? They understand after just a few months. My own thought processes had a lot to do with that and what I believed about myself in regards to Ryan's death. Early on I believed I was more responsible than I actually was.

We all make choices of what to believe. About ourselves, about our families, our friends, life, and about the other person in any given situation. Evaluating my beliefs took a long time to work through. It was a slow, painstaking, exhausting process of holding each belief up to the light and comparing it to scripture and what God says about it.

Add in how we were raised to believe things that might not have been true. We all have inherently held beliefs we don't even realize we have:

> things our parents taught us
>
> things we didn't understand as children
>
> things we misunderstood

My husband Brad is a big part of my healing. He loved me unconditionally and patiently helped me to learn to trust myself. God has brought me this far for a reason. I believe the reason is so I can tell my story.

I could never have dreamed of the restoration and beauty my life would hold once again. Those years—the past, the heartache, pain, joy, gain, all of it—those years with Ryan were his gift to me.

These present years are my gift to Ryan.

Epilogue

Rachel Swanson was one of the last students of Washington High School to interact with Ryan the day he robbed the bank. She has written to Noel and me over the years since. A vivacious and compassionate woman who helped us stay connected to what would have been Ryan's future, she was the perfect person to draw this story out of me.

Writing this story with her has been a monumental learning process. I always knew Ryan had a greater purpose in life. I think I can safely say that in putting all the pieces of the puzzle together to write this story we found treasures we think Ryan wanted to leave to humanity.

It is our greatest prayer that God will use Ryan's story to meet you right where you are in your own personal pain, take your hand, and lead you to find a personal relationship with the God who created you.

So much has unfolded since I put my hand in God's over nineteen years ago. Thank you for allowing me to share my story. Since I started the process of putting this story in print with Rachel, we have both watched God at work. Everyone who knew Ryan could tell his or her own version of this story.

But *this* telling is what God wanted to draw out of the deepest part of my heart.

To the reader, If you are personally struggling with feelings of worthlessness or the lack of purpose in your life; if you are thinking or have thought about suicide, you need to know there are people who love you. And the pain they would feel over your death is beyond anything you could imagine. Their pain would match or exceed my own.

Some people may think they don't have someone who loves them deeply, perhaps because of a fractured relationship with parents or friends who leave them feeling unloved. But there is a heavenly Father who created you and has the capacity to love greater than any human being who ever existed. The Father wants you to know the depth of His love. It runs deep. It is completely unconditional. Can you imagine that kind of love? Can you hear His voice calling you to come near and receive His offer of unconditional love?

Since my son's death, God orchestrated even more healing than I could have imagined.

One day I waited nervously at my church for Troy the police officer to arrive. Rachel had coordinated the meeting between him, Noel, and me. I fumbled with the gift and card I had painstakingly chosen for this occasion. When he walked into the room we immediately hugged, relieving years of tension.

We had a long discussion about the day our lives took a drastic turn and the after-effects that followed. I believe Troy needed to hear that we did not blame him for Ryan's death. The moment was beautiful and meaningful. It was amazing to think of all the time spent in the dry desert in order for this culmination of tears and love. I am thankful to Troy for being willing to talk to us. Our time together provided additional healing to all of us. I felt honored to meet this man whose greatest desire was to make Noel and me feel better.

I feel peace with God and peace with myself. Time and time again my heart turns toward Ephesians 2:14 which says: "For He Himself is our Peace." God is our peace.

In all of my striving to be the person I thought I should be, I missed God's call to my heart to rest. To be still. To allow Him to be my peace.

I now know that no matter what you've gone through or are going through, He can be your peace too.

WORDS FROM RACHEL

What an honor it was when Dawn asked me to help draw out her story of healing seventeen years after Ryan's death. What a privilege! What a responsibility! Throughout our working relationship I began to realize the extent of the healing that had happened in her life. This healing had been allowed to occur, not in spite of, but *because of* her great loss. Without my realizing it, beginning to put her story into words on a crisp blank page began a great healing within me as well.

I'm no stranger to loss. One June afternoon as she handled the items in a small keepsake box that were once her son's, I knew I was treading on sacred ground. Ultimately, her story brought me to a place where I could do what she had so bravely done before me. I could name my losses, see the good that has come of them, truly grieve them, and lay them to rest. We never wholly forget our griefs, and it would be a foolish thing to do. From our deepest hurts come our greatest joys, after all.

About the Author

Dawn Vircks lives with her husband, Brad, in Hiawatha, Iowa. She has a passion for helping people find healing, wellness, and relief from pain. Dawn received her massage license from the State of Iowa in 1998 and established a practice specializing in Neuromuscular Therapy and Cranialsacral Therapy. In her spare time you're apt to find her in line skating the trails through Hiawatha or turning laps at the local ice arena with short track speed skates. She loves to hang out with family—especially a new grandson!

If you'd like to schedule a speaking engagement with Dawn, you may email: DawnNMT@mchsi.com

Made in the USA
Monee, IL
07 July 2026

56550377R00066